Hyde & Closer

HYDE & CLOSER

Volume 2
Shonen Sunday Edition

Story and Art by
HARO ASO

Original Japanese edition "JUHOU KAIKIN!! HYDE AND CLOSER"
published by SHOGAKUKAN Inc.

English Adaptation/AJ Glasser, HC language Solutions, Inc.
Translation/Labaaman, HC language Solutions, Inc.
Touch-up & Lettering/Annaliese Christman
Design/Hidemi Sahara
Editor/Jann Jones, Yuki Murashige

VP, Production/Alvin Lu
VP, Sales & Product Marketing/Gonzalo Ferreyra
VP, Creative/Linda Espinosa
Publisher/Hyoe Narita

Printed in Canada

Published by VIZ Media, LLC
P.O. Box 77010
San Francisco, CA 94107

10 9 8 7 6 5 4 3 2 1
First printing, October 2010

viz
media

www.viz.com

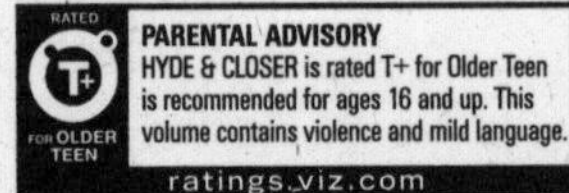
RATED
T+
FOR OLDER TEEN
PARENTAL ADVISORY
HYDE & CLOSER is rated T+ for Older Teen is recommended for ages 16 and up. This volume contains violence and mild language.
ratings.viz.com

SHONEN SUNDAY

WWW.SHONENSUNDAY.COM

Hyde & Closer

2

Story & Art by

Haro Aso

Hyde & Closer
2

Table of Contents

Act 8: Silhouette (1) 5
Act 9: Silhouette (2) 23
Act 10: Silhouette (3) 41
Act 11: Silhouette (4) 59
Act 12: Idle Talk (1) 79
Act 13: Idle Talk (2) 97
Act 14: Puppet (1) 115
Act 15: Puppet (2) 135
Act 16: Puppet (3) 153
Act 17: Puppet (4) 171

What's going on…

Shunpei Closer is an average… well, less-than-average, middle school student who finds himself the target of dark sorcerers.

One day, a suspicious-looking mailman delivers a stuffed monkey toy to Shunpei. The monkey carries a death curse that brings it to life to attack him with knives. Hyde—a stuffed teddy bear left to Shunpei by his grandfather—saves Shunpei from the curse and reveals a shocking truth.

Shunpei's missing grandfather is actually the Sorcerer King! Because Shunpei is part of his bloodline, whoever eats his heart gains the bloodline's unimaginable power. Hyde is a curse created by the Sorcerer King to protect Shunpei!

Now sorcerers around the world are out for Shunpei's blood. What powerful new enemy awaits him next…?!

!
WHO ARE YOU ?!
KKASH
KLIK
WHAT GANG ARE YOU WITH?!
Act 8 Silhouette 1

YOU'RE PUTTING YOUR LIFE ON THE LINE FOR SOME GIRL YOU DON'T EVEN KNOW! YOU GOT A SCREW LOOSE!
WHAT-EVER! JUST GET HIM!

YOU'VE GONE BEYOND THE BOUNDS OF HUMAN-ITY...
...VERMIN LIKE YOU DON'T HAVE A SPECK OF HONOR.

EVEN HELL...

...ISN'T PUNISHMENT ENOUGH FOR YOU ALL.

RAAAAAH
KRACK
ARGH
SMASH
BOOM
POW
HAH
SNAP
AHHHHH
KRUSH
KURLS

THIS "JIN TAKAKURA" IS ONE TOUGH HOMBRE.
KRASH
AHHHHH
SNAP
KRUSH
HYDE, THIS IS A TV SHOW. IT'S JUST A BUNCH OF ACTORS.

PEOPLE LIKE THAT DON'T EXIST IN REAL LIFE.
I'D HAVE DITCHED THE GIRL AND RUN.
DON'T BE A COWARD, SHUN-BOY.
A REAL MAN...
...ALWAYS THINKS OF HIMSELF LAST.
KURLS

Act 8
Silhouette ①

YEAH, BUT...
!
YOU KNOW, SHUN-BOY...
THERE'S SOMETHING I GOTTA GIVE YA.
HUH?
WHAT?
GET THE ZIPPER ON MY BACK.
YOUR ZIPPER?
O-OK...
ZIP
RUSTLE
!

WHAT'S... THIS?
KLINK

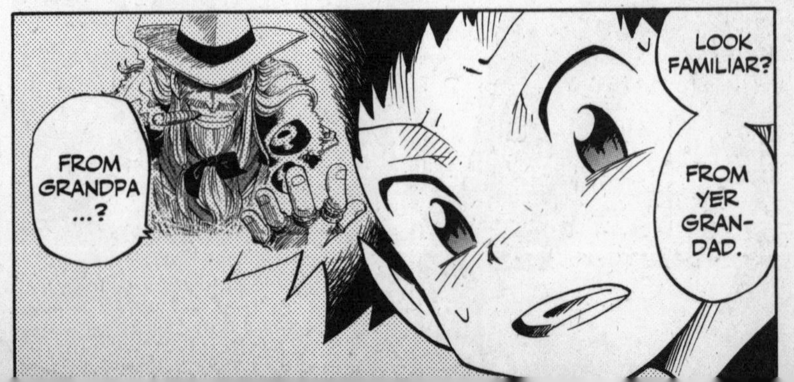
LOOK FAMILIAR?
FROM YER GRAN-DAD.
FROM GRANDPA...?

THE SPELL YA BEEN USING IS CALLED AN "ENTRY BARRIER."
...YOU ARE NOT ALLOWED HERE!
KRACKLE

IT'S AMAZING THAT YA CAN BUILD A BARRIER WITH STATION-ARY...
...BUT WITH "BARRIER STONES" ...

...YER "ENTRY BARRIER" SPELL WILL BE BETTER.

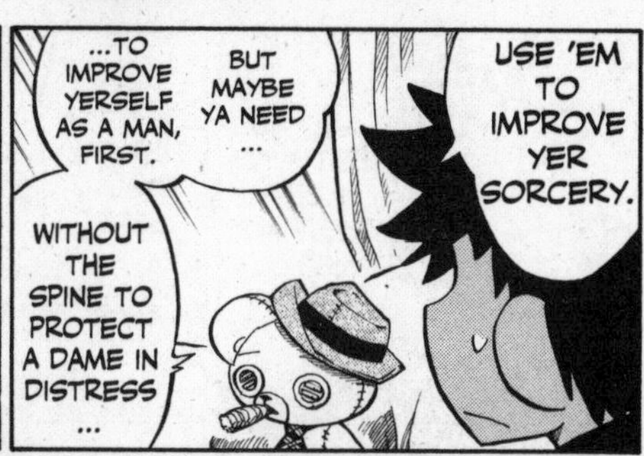
USE 'EM TO IMPROVE YER SORCERY.
BUT MAYBE YA NEED ...
...TO IMPROVE YERSELF AS A MAN, FIRST.
WITHOUT THE SPINE TO PROTECT A DAME IN DISTRESS ...

... YER NEVER GONNA BE POPULAR WITH GIRLS.
TH- THAT'S NONE OF YOUR BUSI-NESS!
GRRR

!
AW, SHOW'S OVER.
YA MADE ME MISS THE BEST PART.
TOO BAD, HYDE ...
... UNLESS THERE'S A RERUN, YOU'LL NEVER SEE IT!
END
NYA

SHORT-SIGHTED, SHUN-BOY!
I KNEW SOME-THING LIKE THIS WOULD HAPPEN ...

...SO I TAPED IT.
WHEN DID YOU LEARN TO DO THAT!
LET'S WATCH IT AGAIN, SHUN-BOY!
THE WHOLE THING ?!
GIVE ME A BREAK
CHIRP
CHIRP

AHHHH!

I OVER-SLEPT!

TMP TMP TMP

HYDE MADE ME WATCH THAT SHOW THREE TIMES!
THIS IS AWESOME!
I LOVE IT!
I DIDN'T GET TO BED 'TIL REALLY LATE!

AND HE GETS TO KEEP SLEEPING!
SO NOT FAIR!
SNOOZE

HEY, LADY!
!
PEEEEK
WHAT'S YOUR PROB-LEM?!

YOUR DUMB DOG BARKED AT THE BOSS HERE...
...AND MADE HIM SPILL ICE CREAM ON HIMSELF!

I-I'M SORRY ...
YIP
YIP

IF APOLOGIES WORKED, WE WOULDN'T NEED COPS! RIGHT?!
WHAT ARE YOU LOOKING AT?!

AHHH! WHAT SHOULD I DO?!
WHY'D I HAVE TO RUN INTO TROUBLE FIRST THING IN THE MORNING!

I WANNA HELP, BUT... SORRY!
THERE'S NOTHING I CAN DO!
HEY! WHAT ARE YOU DOING ?!
JUMP
!
HUH ?!
WHO'RE YOU?!

YOU'RE JUST WHINING ...
...ABOUT A CHIHUAHUA AND SOME ICE CREAM.
YOU'RE PETTY AND YOU GOT NO GUTS!
SHE'S MY CLASS-MATE...
... URYU ?!
YOU CALL YOURSELF YAKUZA?! PICKING ON REGULAR PEOPLE?!
WHAT'D YOU SAY?!
WHO DO YOU THINK YOU'RE TALKING TO?!
THIS IS GETTING CRAZY!
PNNNT
KEEP TALK-ING...
...AND WE'LL DRUG YOU UP AND DROWN YOU!
YOU'RE CLUELESS.

RUMBLE
YOU'VE GONE BEYOND THE BOUNDS OF HUMANITY...
...VERMIN LIKE YOU DON'T HAVE A SPECK OF HONOR.
RUMBLE
HUH...?!
W-WHAT THE...?

HELL...
BOOM
...ISN'T PUNISHMENT ENOUGH FOR YOU ALL.

S-SHE...
...SHE'S ACTING OUT THE TV SHOW!
RUMBLE
!
SCHWAA
KLICK
911

HELLO, POLICE?
SOME GUYS ARE HARASSING A WOMAN IN FRONT OF ME.
YES, THE ADDRESS IS...
WHAT'S WITH THIS BRAT?!
WHAT A HUGE PAIN!!
LET'S SPLIT!
TMP TMP

!
U-UM...

...THANK YOU SO MUCH.
YOU DON'T NEED TO THANK ME.
WAAAA

I JUST DID WHAT I THOUGHT WAS RIGHT.
GLEAM

GRRR
YAAAA

G-GOOD MORNING, URYU...!
YOU'RE CLOSER, RIGHT? FROM SCHOOL...

WHAT'S WITH YOU?
SHE WAS IN TROUBLE AND YOU JUST *STOOD* THERE!

YOU'RE A TERRIBLE PERSON!
OWCH
UGH
W-WELL ...
...I WAS UP AGAINST ...
HM
PH
WHATEVER. DON'T MAKE EXCUSES.
I HATE PEOPLE WHO DON'T HAVE HONOR!
DON'T FOLLOW ME! YOUR COWARDICE MIGHT BE CONTAGIOUS!
I CAN'T HELP IT... I HAVE TO GO TO SCHOOL TOO...

DOH
SIGH
I GUESS I'M JUST NOT COOL ...

HM ...?
I COMPLETELY FORGOT ...
...I'M ALREADY LATE!
I-A

JUST IN TIME!
SWIFF

MORNING, TATSUMI!
MORNING!
WHY ARE YOU SO LOUD IN THE MORNING, URYU?
TARDY
YOU'RE JUST TOO QUIET!
HEY, DID YOU SEE?!
YESTERDAY'S "YAKUZA CHIVALRY WORLD DOMINATION!"

HE CHARGES IN ALL BY HIMSELF TO SAVE A DAMSEL IN DISTRESS!
HE'S SO TOUGH, SO STRONG, AND HE ALWAYS DOES THE RIGHT THING! JIN TAKAKURA IS ALWAYS SO TOTALLY AWESOME!
ALL GUYS SHOULD BE LIKE THAT!
THERE SHE GOES AGAIN, THAT YAKUZA FANGIRL.
NOBODY CAN STOP HER WHEN SHE GETS LIKE THAT ...

MY DREAM IS TO PLAY THE PART OF JIN TAKAKURA'S WIFE AND SUPPORT HIM BEHIND THE SCENES!
PREPARE TO DIE!
FOR MY DREAM, I'LL REHEARSE EVERY DAY!
SWASH
DRAMA CLUB SCENE
URYU IS SO WEIRD.
YUP

COMPARED TO JIN, WHAT CLOSER DID TODAY ...
GLARE
UGH!
GULP
WHAT'S THAT, URYU? WHAT HAPPENED WITH YOU AND SHUNPEI?
NOTH-ING!
FEH
I DUNNO WHAT YOU DID...
...BUT URYU REALLY SEEMS TO HATE YOU, SHUNPEI!
HAHAHA
AWWW
...

DING DONG

OK, SHUN-PEI.
I'M LEAVING WITHOUT YOU.
HUH? WHY?
CUZ, YOU'VE GOT CLEANUP DUTY.

Friday Cleanup
Uryu, Closer

ACK!
SEE YOU TOMORROW.

THUMP
GAZE

WHAT'S WITH YOU?
I ALREADY PUT NOTES IN THE CLASS JOURNAL.

WE JUST HAVE TO TAKE OUT THE TRASH, SO LET'S GO.
BUT...

...DON'T STAND TOO CLOSE TO ME.
I DON'T WANNA CATCH YOUR COWARD COOTIES.
SWIFF
WHAM!!
ARGH

COME ON!
WAIT, URYU!
SNOOZE

STOMP

HEH HEH ...

KL
ICK

HEY THERE!
!

VISITORS AREN'T ALLOWED ON SCHOOL GROUNDS.
WHAT ARE YOU DOING HERE?!

CAN'T YOU TELL?
I HAVE BUSINESS HERE.

SEEMS DODGY ...
COME ON, PAL...YOU CAN TELL ME ALL ABOUT IT.
LET'S GO...
GRIP

UGH ...?!
YA
NK

WHO DO YOU THINK YOU'RE TALKING TO...?!
SK-K-TR

EVERYTHING IN THE WORLD GOES MY WAY. GET IT?
SKKTR
STAY OUT OF MY WAY.
YOU ...
SKKTR

... INSO-LENT WORM.

WHA ...?!
A SHADOW ...?!

Electrical Room
SLF
AHHHH!

HEH HEH ...

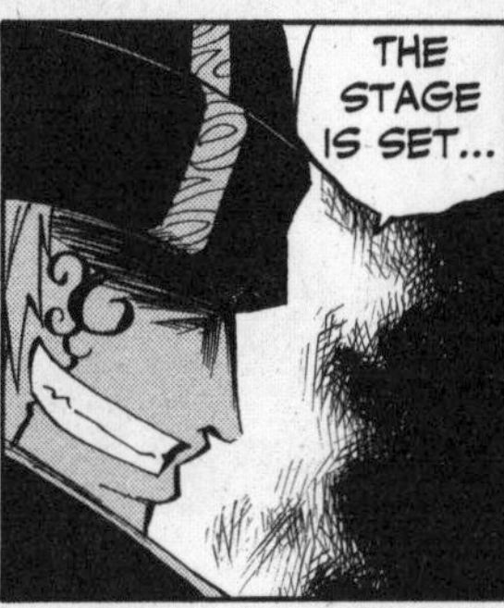
THE STAGE IS SET...

...NOW LET THE HUNT BEGIN!
KLICK

BOOM
?!
HUH?! WHAT'S GOING ON?
A BLACK-OUT?!

GEEZ. SCARED OF A LITTLE BLACKOUT.
WHAT A COWARD ...!
GIVE ME A BREAK ABOUT WHAT HAPPENED THIS MORNING!

NO ...
WAIT.
THE REST OF THE HALLWAY HAS LIGHT ...!

NO WAY ...!
NOW THIS TOO ...?!

"GOD OF DESTRUCTION..."
"...IN ENGULFING DARKNESS."

"FROM THE FOREST OF SCHUNN SCHUYA."
"HAMAN LAKALA, IN YOUR NAME I SUMMON..."

"...UPON CLOSER..."

"...A DEATH CURSE!"

Act 9

Silhouette ②

THIS IS BAD...
THIS IS REALLY BAD!
HYDE ISN'T HERE...

...AND URYU WILL BE IN DANGER IF I'M ATTACKED NOW!
SKKTR

HYDE'S IN THE CLASSROOM ON THE OTHER SIDE OF THE BUILDING.
WHAT SHOULD I DO...?!

WHO IS IT ...?
WHO'S THERE?
!
S-STAY BACK, URYU!
WHAT ARE YOU SO SCARED OF?
YOU'RE PATHETIC.

YO
JUST COME WITH ME!
HEY!
NK
DON'T TOUCH ME!
YOU'LL INFECT ME WITH COWARD!
SKKTR
FORGET ABOUT THAT... WE GOTTA GET OUT OF HERE ...

SKKTK

HUH?

PLIP

CLOSER ...?
!
WHAT HAPPENED TO YOUR ARM?!
PLIP

SHINK

...?!

WHAT THE?!
WHAT'S GOING ON?!

A- AHHH!
GUSH!!
AHHHH!

WE HAVE TO STOP THE BLEED-ING!
UGH... AH...!

HEH HEH...
HEY, GUYS...

...YOU WANNA PLAY "SHADOW TAG?"
?!

SKKTR
IT'S SORT OF LIKE REGULAR "TAG."
BUT INSTEAD OF TAGGING SOMEONE, YOU JUST STEP ON THEIR SHADOW.
SKKTR
PEOPLE WORRY ABOUT BEING CHASED BY THEIR OWN SHADOW.
YOU KNOW WHY?

IT'S BECAUSE YOUR SHADOW...
...IS ANOTHER PART OF YOUR SOUL.
SKKTR
IT'S THE VULNERABLE PART OF YOUR SOUL.

MY CURSE ATTACKS YOUR SHADOWS...
..."BLOODY WAYANG."

I AM SEYABDI!
BY THE HAND OF MY MASTER, BUGS...
A SHADOW PUPPET COME TO LIFE!

I MAY LOOK LIKE A FLAT LITTLE DOLL...
...BUT MY SHADOW IS MY REAL BODY!

AS LONG AS WE BOTH HAVE SHADOWS...
...YOU'LL BE COMPLETELY POWERLESS ...

...AS I TORTURE YOU TO DEATH!
A C-CURSE ...?!
HOLD ON...!
IS THIS A JOKE ?!

I CAN'T DO THIS...
...I NEED HYDE.

IT'S HARD ENOUGH PROTECTING MYSELF.
THERE'S NO WAY I CAN PROTECT URYU TOO...!

WELL ...
...IF YOU SPACE OUT LIKE THAT.
!
SWAA

I'LL TEAR YOU TO PIECES!
SHWING
AHH!
JMP

CLOSER! GET UP!
WE HAVE TO RUN!
STING
AGH ...!

TMP TMP
HEH HEH ...
GOOD. IT'S ONLY FUN WHEN YOU PUT UP A FIGHT...
NOW THE HUNT IS ON.

LET'S HAVE SOME FUN!
TMP

WHAT IS THAT THING?!
TMp TMp
WHAT'S GOING ON HERE?!
...
DO YOU REALLY...
...HAVE SOMETHING TO DO WITH THAT MONSTER?!

WHAT'S THIS ABOUT?!
TELL ME!
I JUST...

UGH...

?!

WHAT HAPPENED?!
HANG IN THERE!

PLUP
!

HE'S HURT BAD!
WE'VE GOT TO GET HIM TO A HOSPITAL FAST!

DID HE...
...DO THIS TOO?

INDEED.
TUp
I DID...!
!

T
Up
THE OLD MAN WAS INSOLENT TO TELL MASTER BUGS TO STOP.

HE WAS BEING ANNOYING, SO I STABBED HIM!
HEH HEH...

...!
JUST FOR THAT?!

WHAT'S YOUR PROB-LEM?!
HOW COULD YOU DO SUCH A THING?!
YOU MON-STER!
U...
URYU ...?!

HUH ...?!
WATCH YOUR MOUTH!
WHO DO YOU THINK YOU'RE TALKING TO?!

I'LL CUT YOU UP, WOMAN!
WHAT DO YOU THINK YOU ARE?!
BZZZ
!

I'VE MADE UP MY MIND.
I'LL KILL THE WOMAN FIRST...!
YOU IRRITATE ME SO MUCH...

...I JUST HAVE TO HEAR YOU SCREAM IN AGONY!
SHHVR
...!

NO ...!
DON'T ...!
LEAVE URYU OUT OF THIS ...!

SHWIP

AHHH!
URYU!
TMP
PLUP
I'M OK... JUST A SCRATCH ...!
GLARE

WHY ?!
WHY ARE YOU DOING THIS?!
IT'S ME YOU WANT, RIGHT ?!
LEAVE EVERYONE ELSE OUT OF THIS!

YOU'RE TELLING ME WHAT TO DO?
HOW ARROGANT.
LISTEN UP, YOU MISERABLE WORMS!
I KILL ANYONE I DON'T LIKE!
AND I AM GOING TO ENJOY KILLING THE GIRL!

EVERYTHING IN THE WORLD GOES MY WAY!
WHEN YOU'RE DEAD AND MASTER BUGS OBTAINS THE POWER OF CLOSER...
AND THEN...
...I'LL BE EVEN STRONGER!

...NO ONE WILL EVER DEFY ME AGAIN!

GRRP
OH, SO...
...I'M BEING ARROGANT ...?!
GRNNO

FIRST, I'LL SLICE OFF BOTH HER LEGS...
...THEN I'LL MAKE HER CRAWL!
TM
JMP
CLOSER?!
KLINK
SKASS
TTER

THIS IS MY DOMAIN...
...I SAY LIGHT...

...IS NOT ALLOWED TO COME IN HERE!
!
POOF

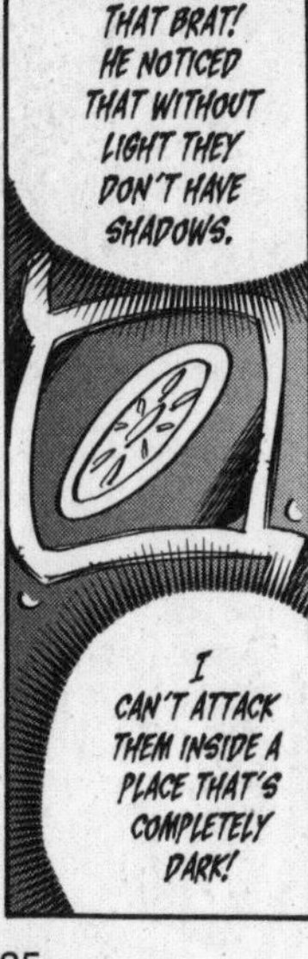
THAT BRAT! HE NOTICED THAT WITHOUT LIGHT THEY DON'T HAVE SHADOWS.
I CAN'T ATTACK THEM INSIDE A PLACE THAT'S COMPLETELY DARK!

HMPH!
TMp
TMp

THEY ARE GONE!
WHERE'D THEY GO?!
JMp

!

OH NO!
THEY'RE GOING OUTSIDE!

I KNEW IT!

THE SUN'S GOING DOWN, SO THERE'RE PLENTY OF SHADOWS TO HIDE IN.
YOU CAN GET AWAY!

NO...!
HOW COULD I LET THIS HAPPEN?!

IF WE HURRY AND GET HELP...
...WE CAN SAVE THE JANITOR TOO!

C'MON, CLOSER!
TMp

I'M NOT GOING ...!

YOU GO SOME-PLACE SAFE.

HUH ...?!
IF I DON'T STAY AND BEAT HIM...
...ANYONE WHO COMES TO HELP THAT OLD GUY...
...COULD GET HURT...!
CLOSER ...?

BEFORE ...
...I JUST FOUGHT BECAUSE I WAS SCARED OF DYING.
BUT NOW IT'S DIFFER-ENT!

IF HE GETS HIS HANDS ON THE CLOSER BLOOD-LINE...
...HE'LL HURT EVEN MORE PEOPLE ...
PLIP
...LIKE YOU, URYU.

I CAN'T ...
...LET THAT HAPPEN!
CLO ...
... SER ...
TH-THUMP

HEH HEH!
SO YOU THREW AWAY YOUR CHANCE TO ESCAPE.
YOU THINK YOU CAN BEAT ME?!

SO...
... INSOLENT!

...
I ONLY HAVE A FEW "BARRIER STONES" LEFT.
I DON'T THINK THE SAME MOVE WILL WORK TWICE...!

NOW WHAT...?!

TOMP
STILL SLOW ON YER FEET, BOY?!
!

BUT YER RIGHT, SHUN.
SPOKEN LIKE A REAL MAN!

HYDE...!

ANOTHER ONE...?!
DON'T WORRY, URYU. HYDE'S ON OUR SIDE.
HOWDY, LITTLE LADY!
WHAT ...?!
UHH... I'LL EXPLAIN LATER...!
LET'S GET THIS OVER WITH, SHUN-BOY!
YEAH!

"TEXAS CHAIN-SAW!"

BZZ

BZZ BZZ BZZ BZZ

VROOM

SO YOU'RE THE BODYGUARD THEY MENTIONED.
YOU WANNA GET IN MY WAY TOO...?
INSOLENT BEAR!

SO YOU'RE THE BODYGUARD THEY MENTIONED.
YOU WANNA GET IN MY WAY TOO?
INSOLENT BEAR!
Act 10 Silhouette 3
YA GOT A BIG HEAD FOR A SMALL GUY.
I'LL BEAT SOME SENSE...
...INTO IT FOR YA...!

Act 10 Silhouette ③

WHAT IS "WAYANG KULIT"?

WAYANG KULIT IS TRADITIONAL SHADOW PUPPET THEATER IN INDONESIA. RECORDS SHOW THAT IT DATES BACK TO THE TENTH CENTURY. WAYANG MEANS "SHADOW," AND KULIT MEANS "SKIN." AS THE NAME SUGGESTS, THE PUPPETS ARE USUALLY MADE FROM WATER BUFFALO HIDE. THE STORIES ARE TYPICALLY DRAWN FROM THE CLASSICAL EPIC POETRY OF THE "MAHABHARATA" AND THE "RAMAYANA." PERFORMANCES CAN LAST MORE THAN EIGHT HOURS.

LET'S GO, PUNK!
TMP
TMP
HEH HEH.
NO GOOD...

MY SHADOW WILL REACH YOU BEFORE YOU REACH ME!

HYDE!
WATCH OUT FOR SEYABDI'S SHADOW!
IT'LL ATTACK YOUR OWN SHADOW. THAT'S HIS CURSE POWER!

IF YOU BOTH CAST SHADOWS, YOU CAN'T GET CLOSE TO SEYABDI!
ZOOM
!
HMPH!
A CREEPY TRICK LIKE THAT...
...SUITS A PUPPET LIKE YA!
SHWING
SO I'LL JUST...
KRASH

...COVER MY SHADOW!

!

AWE-SOME, HYDE!
NOW YOU CAN GO RIGHT UP TO HIM AND ATTACK! GET HIM!

HEH HEH ...

NOT SO FAST!
FLIK

FLASH
!

HEH HEH...!
I CAN SEE YOUR SHADOW.
LET ME SHOW YOU MINE!
SLASH
HYDE!

W-WHAT JUST HAPPENED...?!
IT'S HIM!
THE SORCERER THAT'S MANIPULATING SEYABDI, BUGS.
HE'S CONTROLLING THE LIGHTS SOMEWHERE IN THE SCHOOL!

UNLESS WE STOP BUGS...
...SEYABDI CONTROLS THE WHOLE BUILDING!

THE ELEC-TRICAL ROOM ...

THAT'S IT! THE ELEC-TRICAL ROOM!
HUH ...?!

THE DRAMA CLUB REHEARSES IN THE AUDITOR-IUM.
I KNOW THERE'S AN ELECTRICAL ROOM BACK THERE THAT CONTROLS THE LIGHTING!

THAT'S WHERE HE IS!

HYDE!
LET'S GO THERE!
!

I'LL GO SHUT OFF ALL THE LIGHTS!
THAT'LL MAKE SEYABDI POWER-LESS!

HEH ...
YER GETTING THE HANG OF THIS, MY BOY.
GUESS HE GOT UNDER YER SKIN.

GOOD TO SEE YA SHOWIN' SOME BACK-BONE!
AIN'T MY STYLE TO TURN THE LIGHTS OUT ON SOME-ONE...
...BUT I OUGHTA GO WITH YA THIS TIME!
HURRY, CLOSER!
THE ELEC-TRICAL ROOM IS THIS WAY!
TMP TMP
URYU ?!
WHAT ARE YOU DOING?!
TMP TMP
YOU GOTTA STAY OUT OF THIS!
TMP
I WANT TO RUN AWAY...
...BECAUSE I'M SCARED!
BUT ...
...HONOR DEMANDS ...
...I STICK BY A FRIEND IN TROUBLE!

YOU'LL EXPLAIN THIS ALL TO ME LATER, RIGHT?!
URYU...

AUDITORI
HERE WE ARE!
WHAM

HURRY!
THE ELECTRICAL ROOM IS OVER THERE!
TMPTMP

HEH HEH HEH...

IT MAKES ME LAUGH...
...WHEN THINGS GO ACCORDING TO PLAN!
HUH?!

EVERYTHING IN THIS WORLD...
...GOES MY WAY.
FLIK

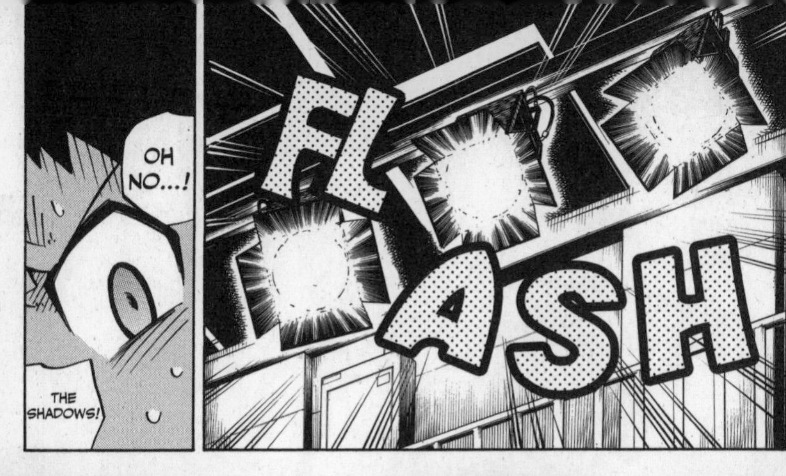
FLASH
OH NO...!
THE SHADOWS!

NOW YOU HAVE COUNTLESS VULNERABLE SHADOWS!

AND I HAVE ENDLESS SHADOWS TO ATTACK THEM WITH!

THIS IS THE TRUE POWER OF "BLOODY WAYANG"!

THE IDEAL STAGE HAS BEEN SET!
HEH HEH ...
NOW FOR THE GRAND FINALE!

THIS WAS HIS PLAN ALL ALONG...!
I BET BUGS IS RIGHT BEHIND THAT DOOR...!
SHOOT!
C'MON, SHUN-BOY.
THAT'S ALL YA GOT?

I'LL KEEP HIM BUSY HERE.
YA GET ON OVER TO THAT ROOM.
HYDE ...!

WE'LL GO WITH YER PLAN THIS TIME.

THIS OLD BEAR'LL JUST SHUT UP AND BELIEVE IN YA.

HUH?!
YOU? KEEP ME BUSY?
SO INSOLENT!
THEY WON'T GET TO MASTER BUGS!
I'LL KILL THE BRAT AND THE GIRL FIRST!
SKREECH
JMP
!

HYDE!
RRRRRV
GRRP
...
LET'S GO, URYU!
WE'LL BE IN HYDE'S WAY IF WE STICK AROUND!
WAIT! WHAT ABOUT HYDE?

COME ON AL-READY!
JUST TRUST HYDE!
!

OK...!
TMP

YOU'RE DETERMINED ...
...TO GET IN MY WAY!
GRRRND

THAT'S A DEATH WISH.
LET ME FULFILL IT FOR YOU!
HSSSA

HA HA ...
DON'T THINK I'LL LAST LONG...
WEEE

I'M COUNTING ON YA, SHUN!
Electrical Room

WHAM!!

HUFF
HUFF

HEH HEH ...
I DIDN'T THINK YOU'D MAKE IT THIS FAR.

THE SWITCH YOU WANT IS RIGHT HERE.
BUT DO YOU REALLY THINK TWO LITTLE KIDS CAN TAKE ON A GROWN MAN?
HEH HEH ...
I COULD KILL YOU MYSELF.
SHUK
BUT TO GET THE POWER OF SORCERER KING CLOSER ...
...I HAVE TO USE A CURSE ON YOU.
THE DOLL MUST TEAR OUT YOUR HEART FOR ME.

SO FOR NOW, I'LL KEEP YOU ALIVE...
TM
P
...AND JUST CUT YOUR BODY!

SK
ATT
ER

THIS IS MY DOMAIN.
SWUU

HEH HEH ...!
DON'T YOU KNOW ANY OTHER SPELLS?!
IS THAT PITIFUL "ENTRY BARRIER" ALL YOU CAN DO?

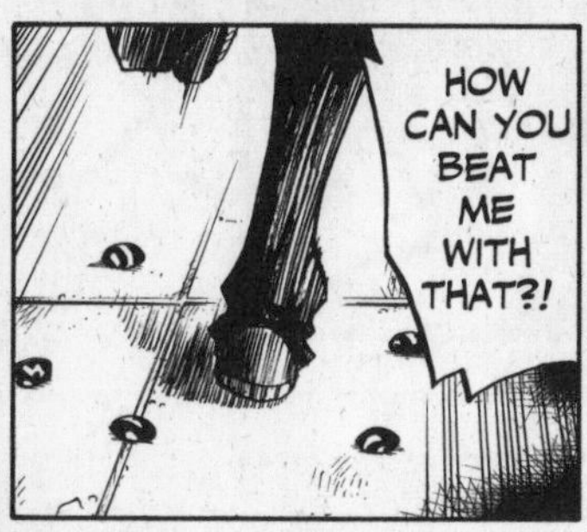
HOW CAN YOU BEAT ME WITH THAT?!

I SAY YOU...
?!

...ARE NOT ALLOWED TO ESCAPE!

KRACKLE

HUH ?!
WHAT IS THIS ...?!
KRACKLE
A SPELL THAT RESTRICTS ITS TARGET.

A "CHAIN SEAL" SPELL ?!
THIS CAN'T BE!
WHEN DID HE LEARN TO DO THAT?!

I CAN KEEP PEOPLE OUT OF MY DOMAIN, SO...
...IF I REVERSE IT...

...IT MEANS I CAN KEEP YOU IN!

DOOM

WHAT ...?!
HE FIGURED THAT OUT HIMSELF SO QUICKLY?!
THE LITTLE BRAT...
HE LEARNS FAST!
I'M SO GLAD THAT WORKED.
THUMP
THUMP

I DON'T REALLY GET WHAT'S GOING ON...
...BUT YOU'RE AMAZING, CLOSER ...!

HE'LL STAY PUT FOR NOW!
UGH ...!
AWE-SOME!
NOW, LET'S TURN OFF THE LIGHTS!

YEAH!
GRR

?!
...!
WHAT ...?!

KRAK
KRAK
AN "ENTRY BARRIER"?
HEH HEH ...
OH, ARE YOU SURPRISED ...?
I CAN USE A BEGINNER'S SPELL TOO.

EVERY-THING IN THIS WORLD GOES MY WAY!
AFTER I RIP THAT BEAR UP...
...I'LL DEAL WITH YOU TWO. SLOWLY!

EVERY-THING IN THIS WORLD ...
... GOES MY WAY!
Act 11 Silhouette ④

...!
WHAT ...?!
KR
ACKLE
AN "ENTRY BARRIER"?

NOW YOU'RE OUT OF OPTIONS!
AFTER I RIP THAT BEAR UP...
...I'LL DEAL WITH YOU TWO. SLOWLY!

Act 11
Silhouette ④

DOOOM
HUFF
HUFF

HEH HEH...

LOOK AT YOU. WOUNDED AND TORN.

YOU CAN BARELY STAND.
HEH HEH... YOU LOOK PATHETIC.

MASTER BUGS KNOWS ALL!
NO MATTER HOW HARD YOU FIGHT...
...THAT KID'S PLAN WILL FAIL...
...AND YOU WILL DIE HERE IN VAIN!

SHUT YER TRAP, PUNK!
WHAT?!
YOU AND ME BOTH AIN'T GOT MUCH TIME LEFT.
DON'T WASTE YER BREATH.
KILL ME IF YA GET THE CHANCE.
WHEEZE
WHEEZ

HOW CAN YOU...
...BE SO ARROGANT!
BUT UNDER-ESTIMATE MY BOY SHUN...
...AND YER ASKIN' FER TROUBLE!

NOW WHAT, KIDS?
HEH HEH ...

HA HA HA HA!
ALL YOU CAN DO IS WATCH!
NO...
BUT WE MADE IT THIS FAR...
HEH HEH ...

YOUR BEAR ISN'T DOING SO GREAT.
I GIVE HIM TWO MINUTES, TOPS... MAYBE JUST ONE.

DAMN IT!!

THE SWITCH IS RIGHT IN FRONT OF ME...!
I WAS SO CLOSE ...
DAMN ...!

CLOSER ...

GLARE

STOP FEELING SORRY FOR YOURSELF.
THINK!

HYDE'S OUT THERE FIGHTING ON HIS OWN BECAUSE HE TRUSTS YOU!
WE CAN'T GIVE UP NOW!

URYU ...
THINK!
THINK WHAT YOU CAN DO!
FIGHT TO THE END.

YOU CAN GIVE UP...

... *AFTER* THAT JERK KILLS YOU!

HEH HEH.
I ADMIRE THAT SPIRIT.

BUT WHAT CAN YOU DO?!
YOU CAN'T TOUCH THE SWITCH.
YOU CAN'T ERASE SEY-ABDI'S SHADOW!

...!
ERASE ...
...HIS SHADOW ...?

THAT'S IT!
CLOSER! FOLLOW ME!
TMP
TMP
?
HUH ...?!
WHAM

THE DRAMA CLUB...
...PROP CLOSET ...?
WHAT ARE WE DOING HERE ...?
UNK

...!
THIS!

To all drama club members,
Everyone, take your umbrellas home!! Look at how many are here. What are we gonna do with them!?!
-Club President

PLASTIC UMBREL-LAS?

WE NEED TO GO UPSTAIRS IN THE AUDITOR-IUM...
...AND COVER ALL OF THE LIGHTS WITH THESE UMBREL-LAS!
WHAT ?!
BUT... WHAT IS THAT GOING TO DO?!
FWAP

JUST HURRY UP!
TRUST ME!
TMP
KLANG
O-OK!
SLAM
!

HYDE!
SLASH

HEH...
WHAT ARE YA WASTING YER TIME ON NOW, SHUN-BOY?
I'M GETTIN' TIRED OF WAITIN'.
WHEEZ
WHEEZ
HYDE...!
YOU'RE ALL TORN UP...
...BECAUSE OF ME...!

WHAT ARE YOU DOING ?!
HURRY UP, CLOSER!
YOU WANT TO HELP HYDE, RIGHT?!
KLACK

BUT, URYU ...!
HOW WILL THIS STOP SEYABDI?!
FWAP
SOFT LIGHT!
KLACK

"SOFT LIGHT ...?"
IT'S A TECHNIQUE USED IN THEATER AND PHOTO-GRAPHY!
A PARTIALLY TRANSPARENT LAYER WILL DIFFUSE THE LIGHT...
...AND SOFTEN THE SHADOW'S EDGES!

WITH THE LIGHTS SHINING FROM EVERY DIREC-TION...
KLACK
TMP TMP
...WE GET MULTIPLE SHADOWS, BUT THEY'RE NOT VERY DARK.
!
SWUU
HUH ?!
YOU TWO...!
WHAT ARE YOU DOING ?!
KLACK
SO IF WE SOFTEN ALL THE LIGHT IN THE ROOM ...
SWUU
...THE SHADOWS ...
KLACK
...WILL COMPLETELY DISAPPEAR!
!
HEY ...?!
MY DREAM IS TO CO-STAR WITH JIN TAKAKURA!
THAT'S AMAZ-ING!
I DON'T REHEARSE IN DRAMA CLUB FOR NOTHING!
YOU'RE AWE-SOME, URYU!

WE JUST NEED ONE MORE UMBRELLA...
TMP TMP
...ON THAT LAST LIGHT.
HUH ?!
?!

NO!
IT'S SO FAR AWAY!

WHY ...?!
IT WAS RIGHT HERE DURING REHEARSAL YESTERDAY.
SOMEONE MUST HAVE MOVED IT DURING THE DAY!
...
HEH HEH ...
DON'T SCARE ME LIKE THAT ...!
AS IF SUCH A WEAK PLAN WOULD ACTUALLY WORK!

ONE MORE STAB SHOULD FINISH THE BEAR!
JUST STAND THERE AND WATCH.

EVERYTHING IN THE WORLD...
WHEEZ
WHEEZ

ZVIP
...GOES MY WAY!

NO...
...WE GOT SO FAR.

WE WERE SO CLOSE!

IT'S NOT OVER YET, URYU!
!
WE CAN GIVE UP...
TOMP
... AFTER ...

...THAT JERK KILLS US!
JMP
KLACK
CLOSER!

NO!

MY SHADOWS!

SW
UU

ACK!

GRASP

TOMP
EEK!
TWITCH

LOOKS LIKE EVERYTHING IN THE WORLD ...
...DOESN'T GO YER WAY, PUNK.
VRRRRRRR

GOOD THING ...
...AT LEAST YA LEARNED THAT.
TOMP
OK!
H-HOLD ON!
I'M SORRY!

GO MAKE YOURSELF USEFUL...
USEFUL IN HELL! SEE YA, PUNK!
I..
I'M SORRY ...

KRACK

OW! THAT HURTS!
THAT REALLY HURTS!

YOU TWO WENT THROUGH A LOT!
!

BUT WE GOT THE GUY THAT ATTACKED YOU.
YOU'RE SAFE NOW.
OH, ALSO...

...THE JANITOR MADE IT.
HE'LL LIVE.

THAT'S GREAT!
YEAH!

THANK YOU SO MUCH, URYU.
BUT IF SOMETHING LIKE THIS EVER HAPPENS AGAIN...

COULD YOU MAKE A RUN FOR IT?

CALL ME TATSUMI.

SHUNPEI!

DON'T BE SILLY.
I KNOW YOUR SECRET NOW.
THOUGH IT'S HARD TO BELIEVE...
HUH ...?
I PROBABLY CAN'T HELP MUCH...
...BUT TELL ME NEXT TIME YOU'RE IN TROUBLE!

URY-
...UH, TATSUMI.
ACTUALLY, SHUNPEI ...
THERE WAS SOMETHING ELSE I GOT REALLY EXCITED ABOUT TODAY...
HUH?! WHAT'S THAT?

HOW SHOULD I PUT IT?
MASCU-LINE... AND COOL...
...MY IDEAL MAN'S MAN IN ALMOST EVERY WAY...
I...
I THINK I'M IN LOVE...
HUH ?!
T-TATSUMI ?!

...WITH HYDE.
BLUSH
KRUSH
ZZZZZZZ

AWWWW
OH, AND BY THE WAY, SHUNPEI ...
YEAH, TATSUMI ?
I'M WORRIED ABOUT THAT SOR-CERER BUGS.
WHAT IF HE COMES BACK?
I THINK IT'LL BE OK.
?

WHEN THE CORE OF A DOLL IS DESTROYED, THE CURSE FAILS...
...AND REBOUNDS ON THE SORCERER WHO CAST IT.

AFTER ALL THAT BUGS DID...
...I'M SURE HE'S GETTING EXACTLY WHAT HE DE-SERVES.

GET IN THERE!
YOU'LL BE HERE A WHILE!
KREAK

HMPH ...
TELLING ME WHAT TO DO LIKE SOME BIG SHOT...
HOW ARRO-GANT!

WHATEVER! I'LL GET A NEW DOLL SOON...
...AND THEN KILL ALL OF THEM AND TEAR OUT THAT KID'S HEART!
HEH HEH ...

WHAT ARE YOU DOING ?!
HURRY UP AND GET IN THERE!
KLICK

YOWCH
GAH!
W-WHAT'S THAT ?!

H-HEY... WHAT'S WRONG ?
UGH ...!

THROB
ARE YOU OK?
TUP
AHHHHHH!

WHAT HAP-PENED ?!
I DON'T KNOW. HE JUST STARTED SCREAMING ALL OF A SUDDEN.
HUFF
HUFF

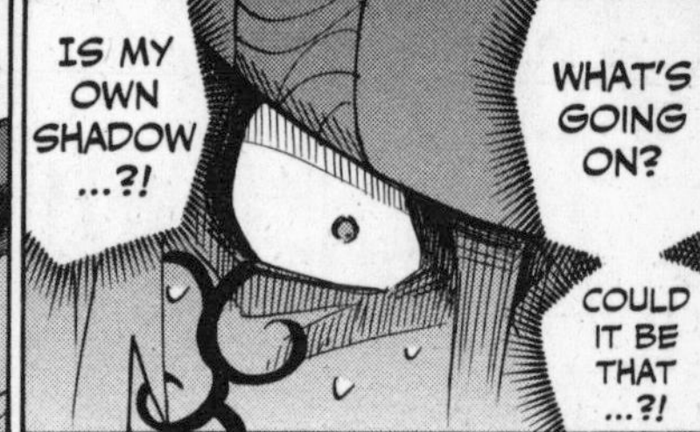
WHAT'S GOING ON?
IS MY OWN SHADOW ...?!
COULD IT BE THAT ...?!

G-GET AWAY...!
DON'T COME NEAR ME!
?

P-PLEASE! PUT ME IN PRISON!
JUST SOME-PLACE WITH NO SHADOWS ...!
ANYWHERE LIGHT CAN'T REACH ME!
ACTUALLY... I DON'T CARE WHERE...!

BUT I WORKED SO HARD THIS TIME!
AWWW
?

Act 12 Idle Talk 1

YAY
YAY

UGH!
KICK

SHUN-PEI!
GET THE BALL!

IT'S ALL YOU!
MAKE THE KICK!
HUH?! ME?!

I'M NOT SCARED!
I'M SO AWE-SOME NOW!
WIF
WIF
WIF

I CAN MAKE THIS SHOT!
AND THEY'LL ALL SEE HOW COOL I AM!
SWING
TOMP

Act 12
Idle Talk ①

KRAACK

HUH ...?
WHAT WAS THAT ?
BOING
BOING

AHHHHHHH!
SWIFFF!!

SIGH ...
THAT WAS LAME ...
... EVEN FOR ME.

HAPPENS ALL THE TIME, EH, SHUN-BOY!
HA HA HA
YOU DON'T GET IT, DO YOU?

IT'S HARD TO BE COOL.
I WISH I WERE LIKE...

... GRANDPA AND YOU, HYDE.
...

SHUN, MY BOY.
YEAH ?

WHAT IS IT...
...THAT MAKES A MAN COOL?

HUH?

...

WHEN I GROW UP...

...I WANT TO BE COOL LIKE GRANDPA!

WHAT MAKES YOU COOL?
I'M NOT SURE.

SMAK
KLUNK
!

ALL RIGHT! I HIT IT!
TLK
TLK
HIT THAT NEXT!

SMAK
KLUNK
YOU GOT IT!

AMAZ-ING!
PRETTY COOL, HUH?!
BUT HITTING EMPTY CANS IS BORING.

LET'S USE YOUR ROBOT!
HUH ...?

N-NO!
NOT THIS!
YOINK

YOU'LL BREAK IT!
AW, C'MON! IT'LL BE FINE!
IT'LL BE SO COOL, YOU'LL SEE!

NO! DON'T!
C'MON! WHAT'S YOUR PROBLEM ?!
JUST GIVE IT TO ME!
SHUN-BOY?

...
-RI!

MI-NORI!
!

WHAT DO YOU WANNA DO TODAY?
LET'S PLAY VIDEO GAMES AT MY HOUSE.
MY PARENTS JUST GOT ME A NEW ONE.
AW, VIDEO GAMES AGAIN?!
LET'S PLAY OUT-SIDE!
BUT ...
...I'M NOT VERY HEALTHY ...
...SO I'M NOT ALLOWED TO PLAY OUTSIDE.
IT'S OK IF IT'S ONLY FOR A LITTLE WHILE.
COOL GUYS DON'T TALK LIKE THAT!
BUT ...
COME ON, LET'S GO!
RACE YOU TO THE PARK!
TMP
O-OK.
TUP TUP

HEY, SHUN-PEI...
!
LET'S GO HOME.
I'M REALLY TIRED...
HUFF
HUFF
HUH ?!
IT'S NOT EVEN THAT LATE YET.
LET'S STAY LONGER.

LET'S CLIMB THAT TREE NEXT!
FIRST ONE THAT GETS TO THE BOTTOM BRANCH IS THE REAL MAN!

...
HUFF
HUFF

HUFF
HUFF
HUFF

JUST A LITTLE MORE...

YOINK

I DID IT! I CLIMBED THE TREE!
PRETTY COOL, HUH?!

COME ON, MINORI! COME UP...
PLOP

MINORI ?!
WHEEZ
WHEEZ

I'M TERRIBLY SORRY, MA'AM.

SHUN HERE DIDN'T KNOW BETTER THAN TO DRAG YOUR BOY AROUND LIKE THAT.

THE DOCTORS TOLD HIM NOT TO OVER-EXERT HIMSELF!

WE GOT LUCKY TODAY!

BUT HE COULD HAVE DIED!

I CANNOT ALLOW...

...MINORI TO PLAY WITH YOUR CHILD ANYMORE!

I'M TERRIBLY ...
... ORRY.

GOTTA TAKE IT EASY, SHUN, MY BOY.
BE MORE CAREFUL NEXT TIME.

I DIDN'T KNOW...
...MINORI WAS SO SICK.
AND GRANDPA...
...YOU ALWAYS SAY BOYS SHOULD PLAY OUTSIDE MORE.
PLAYING AROUND OUTSIDE AIN'T A BAD THING.

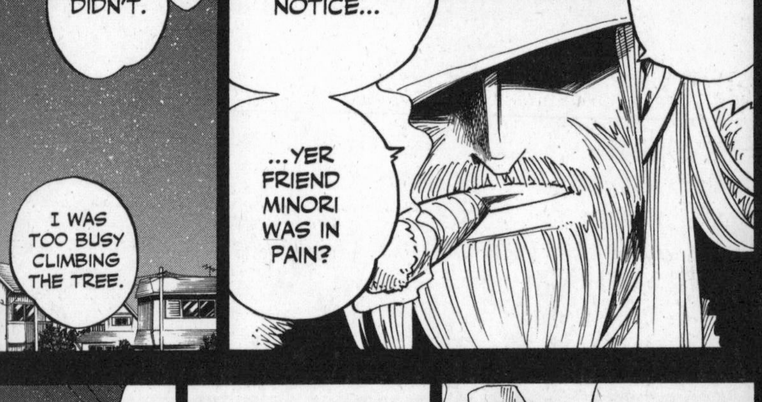
BUT SHUN...
...YA DIDN'T EVEN NOTICE...
...YER FRIEND MINORI WAS IN PAIN?
...
NO. I DIDN'T.
I WAS TOO BUSY CLIMBING THE TREE.

I WANTED MINORI TO THINK I WAS COOL.
GEEZ...
YA DON'T GET IT, SHUN-BOY.

THAT AIN'T BEING COOL.

...

HOW CAN SOMEONE...

...BE COOL?

WELL, SHUN-BOY...

THAT'S SOMETHING YA HAVE TO FIND OUT YERSELF.

IF YA CAN'T FIGURE IT OUT...

...BY THE TIME I'M BACK FROM MY NEXT TRIP, I'LL TELL YA.
GLEAM
WOOSH

AFTER THAT ...
...GRANDPA SENT ONE LAST LETTER FROM AFRICA. AND DISAPPEARED.

NO!
COME ON! IT'S OK!

FP
SHUN-BOY?

HEY, GUYS.
!

LEAVE HIM ALONE.

IF HE DOESN'T WANT TO, YOU CAN'T MAKE HIM.

YOU TALKING TO US?!
SHUT UP, LOSER!
GRR
GRR
SHOOT HIM!
KLICK
AHHHH!
DADADA
CAUTION: NEVER SHOOT BB GUNS AT OTHER PEOPLE.

MAN, THAT WAS COOL!
SIZZLE
FORGET THAT LOUSY OLD ROBOT!
CAUTION: IT'S ACTUALLY NOT COOL TO SHOOT AT PEOPLE.
A- ARE YOU OK?
OW...

U- UM...
THIS ROBOT ...
...IT'S THE LAST THING MY DAD GAVE ME BEFORE HE WENT AWAY.
SO ...
THANK YOU...
...FOR SAVING HIM!
OH...
WOW ...

I'M GLAD THEY DIDN'T BREAK IT.

BUT I GOT BEAT UP BY GRADE SCHOOL-ERS!
HOW LAME IS THAT!
YEAH, REALLY.
HEH
HAHA
HAHAHA
GEEZ...
YA REALLY DON'T GET IT, SHUN-BOY.
HEH

THAT RIGHT THERE... IS WHAT BEING COOL IS ALL ABOUT.

KOALA!
TODAY'S THE DAY! I'M GOING TO EAT YOU ALL UP!
TAS-MANIAN DEVIL!
DON'T YOU TOUCH MY HOUSE!

Act 13 Idle Talk 2

WHATCHA WATCHING, HYDE?
HM? WHAT AM I WATCH-ING?

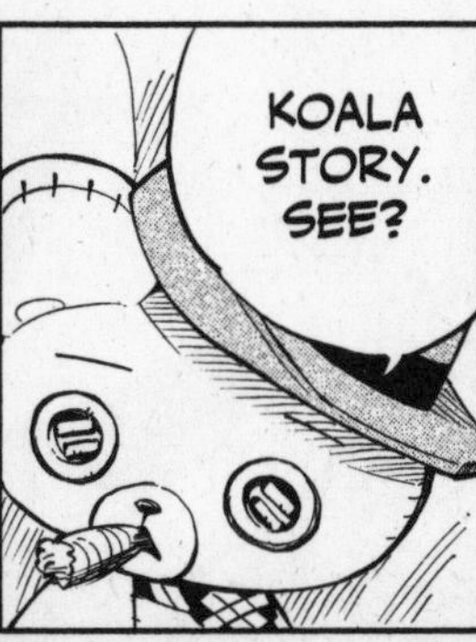
KOALA STORY. SEE?

IT'S INTEREST-ING.
OH, YEAH?

YOU'RE ALWAYS GOING ON ABOUT BEING A REAL MAN OR WHATEVER.
SO WHY DO YOU WATCH LITTLE KIDS' CARTOONS?

Act 13 Idle Talk 2

ZZZZ
ZZZZ

I CAN'T SLEEP!

I SLEEP ALL THE TIME AT SCHOOL, CUZ THERE'S NOTHING ELSE TO DO.
NOW I CAN'T SLEEP AT NIGHT.
NNNN

NOTHING TO DO... GOTTA BE SOMETHING FUN SOME-WHERE...
BLARF
!

WHAT'S THIS?
BLARF

UGH!
SIGH

MAN, I'M TRASHED.
WOBBLE
THOUGHT A DRINK WOULD PICK ME UP, BUT I DRANK TOO MUCH.
HICCUP
HEY, YOU!
HICCUP
HUH?

WHADDYA DOING?
JUMP
WHOA?! WHAT ARE YOU?!

WHAT THE? A STUFFED ANIMAL IS TALKING.

GUESS I'M REALLY DRUNK.
HICCUP
YA SHOULDN'T TOSS YER COOKIES OUTSIDE SOMEBODY'S HOUSE.

HUH?
WHO D'YA THINK YOU'RE TALKING TO?
HICCUP
TUP
TP

I'M A YAKUZA THUG, MAN!
THE INFAMOUS "MAD DOG" TAIZO YAKARA...
...OF THE SANDEI GROUP!
YA GOTTA PROBLEM WITH ME?!

I DON'T CARE IF YOUR NAME IS MAD DOG OR PUKE DOG.
YA GO PUKE SOMEPLACE ELSE, OR I'LL GIVE YA TROUBLE.
VVVVVp
GRRIND
OW! OW!
I-I'M SORRY! I'M SORRY!
NOT BAD...
BUT NOW I'M GONNA GET SERIOUS!
YOWCH
HMPH HMPH
SO YA LIKE TO SHOW OFF, EH?

SORRY, BUT I DON'T GOT TIME TO DEAL WITH YA.
HAVE FUN ON YER OWN NOW, YA HEAR?
TOMP
...
HICCUP
HEY...
WANNA GRAB A DRINK?
?

SUICIDE ASSASSIN?

ODEN

THAT'S RIGHT...
...I'M SUPPOSED TO OFF A BITSUGU GROUP EXECUTIVE TONIGHT.
RUSTLE
THEY'LL PROBABLY LOCK ME UP FOR TEN YEARS...
HUH, A MOVING STUFFED ANIMAL... MAYBE I'M SENILE...

...BUT IF I DO IT RIGHT, I'LL GET A SILVER BADGE WHEN I COME OUT!
HICCUP
THAT AIN'T SOME-THING TO BE PROUD OF...
...BUT I GUESS IT AIN'T EASY BEING A YAKUZA.

JUST SO YOU KNOW! I'M NOT GETTING DRUNK CUZ I'M AFRAID OF KILLIN' SOMEBODY!
YEAH, SURE.

BUT I THOUGHT YAKUZA HIT MEN ...
...WERE ALL YOUNGER GUYS.
!

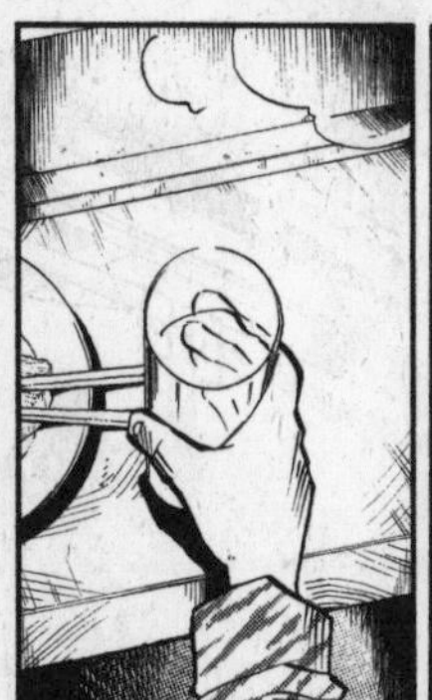

I...
I SUCK AT FIGHTING AND I'M A COWARD, TOO.
EVEN THOUGH I'M GETTING OLD, I'M STILL AT THE BOTTOM.
ODEN

SO FOR ME...
...THIS IS MY LAST CHANCE TO MAKE IT BIG.

LAST CHANCE, EH...?
HEY, POPS. HANPEN FISH-CAKE.
S-SURE ...
GOT SOME DAMES TO IMPRESS, DO YA?
HA! YOU COULD SAY THAT!

I GOT A WIFE AND DAUGHTER.
HICCUP

PLUS, ANOTHER ONE ON THE WAY! TWO KIDS!
...!

WE'RE GETTING POORER BY THE DAY.
I'M THE BREADWINNER SO I GOTTA DO SOMETHING BIG, YOU KNOW!

A FAMILY, EH?
SO...

...YA SHOULDN'T BE OUT RISKING YER NECK.
GET OUT OF THE BUSI-NESS.
!

YOU DON'T GET IT!

I KNOW I'M NOT A GOOD YAKUZA ...
BUT I'M STILL A MAN!
I CAN'T CALL IT QUITS NOW AND FIND SOME OTHER WAY TO LIVE!

THE KIDS THAT JOINED UP AFTER ME KEEP GETTING PROMOTED, WHILE I'M STUCK AT THE BOTTOM. THEY BOSS ME AROUND ...
...AND I'VE JUST BEEN PUTTING UP WITH IT!
IF I QUIT NOW, THE WHOLE GANG'LL LAUGH AT ME!
GOTTA SHOW 'EM ALL UP, THOSE SNOT-NOSED PUNKS!

I CAN'T QUIT NOW!
I GOTTA DO IT! I GOTTA...!
SHAKE

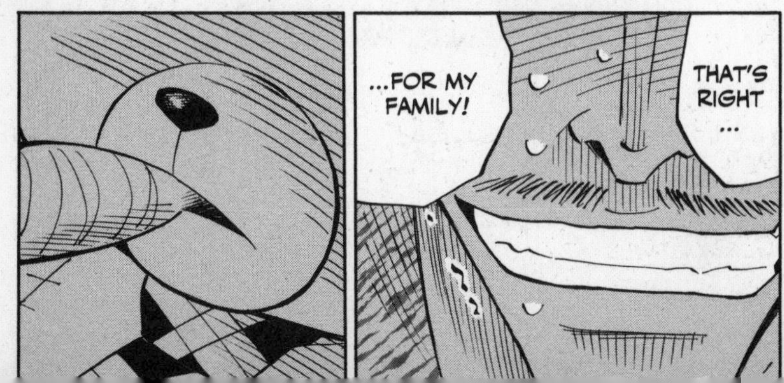
THAT'S RIGHT ...
...FOR MY FAMILY!

YER FAMILY? THAT'S A LOAD OF BULL.

YA THINK THIS MAKES YA A MAN?

THAT'S REAL FUNNY.
WHAT?!

WHAT'D YOU SAY?!
WHAT'S YOUR PROB-LEM?!
ODEN

IF YA REALLY WANT TO PROTECT SOME-THING...
...YA GOTTA LOSE THAT PRIDE...

...AND PROTECT 'EM 'TIL THE DAY YA DIE.
THAT'S WHAT A MAN DOES.
...!

YA AIN'T PROTECTING YER FAMILY.

YER PROTECTING YER STUPID PRIDE.

KRACK
GAH!
YAKARA. YOU'VE BEEN AROUND LONGER THAN US.
YOU GOTTA AT LEAST PULL YOUR OWN WEIGHT.
DAMMIT ...!
I'LL MAKE IT BIG SOMEDAY!

DADDY!

KLUNK

SHUFF

KRUNCH
WHAT ARE YOU DOING, TAIZO?!
!

...!

BOSS JUNIOR ...!
SO YOU LOST YOUR NERVE AGAIN.
WHY AM I NOT SUR-PRISED?

THIS IS WHY YOU CAN'T GET AHEAD, TAIZO!

...
IT'S NOT THAT, SIR.
I JUST ...
...I JUST FIGURED OUT WHAT I REALLY WANT TO PROTECT.

BOSS JUNIOR?
YEAH?

PLEASE ...

...LET ME LEAVE THE GROUP.

WHAT ...?
WHAT DO YOU THINK THE YAKUZA IS?

HUH... OK...
I'LL LET YOU QUIT, TAIZO...!
SWIFF
!

BUT!
ONLY IF YOU CAN ESCAPE ALIVE!
TMP
TMP

...!
AH, GOOD.
NICE AND SIMPLE!
HYAAH
?!

KRACK
UGH!
SMASH
AGH!
SPLAT
ACK!

KRASH
AHHHH!
B-BOSS JUNIOR ?!
SIR!

THAT SHOULD DO FOR HIM.

ANY OF *YOU* PUNKS WANT A PIECE?

DOOM

HUH ...?!
DIDN'T SEE HYDE.
H-HE'S THAT TOUGH?!
AHHHH!
TOMP

TOMP
W-WHAT...
WHAT ARE YOU DOING HERE?

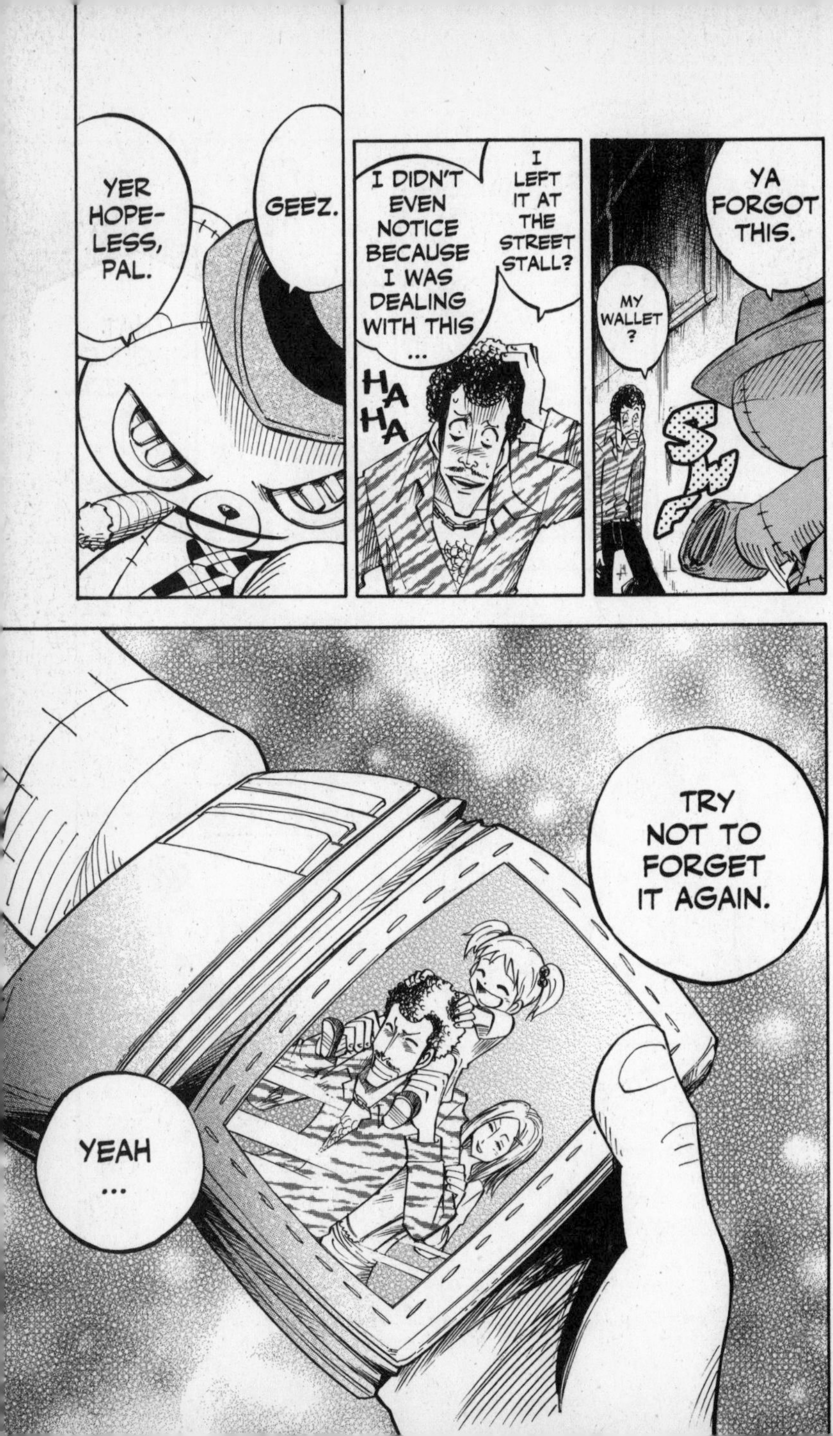

YA FORGOT THIS.

MY WALLET?

I LEFT IT AT THE STREET STALL?

I DIDN'T EVEN NOTICE BECAUSE I WAS DEALING WITH THIS ...

HA HA HA

GEEZ.

YER HOPE-LESS, PAL.

TRY NOT TO FORGET IT AGAIN.

YEAH ...

!

MORE CARTOONS, HYDE?

C'MON, THEY'RE FOR LITTLE KIDS!

YOU THINK SO?

STILL A GOOD STORY ...

AHHH!
NOT AGAIN!
WHY CAN'T I EVER GET KOALA DOWN!

YOU KEEP TRYING ...
I'LL ALWAYS PROTECT MY FAMILY!

GUESS SHUN-BOY'S A BIT TOO YOUNG TO UNDERSTAND ...

Act 14 Puppet 1

PLOT SUMMARY

I'M SHUNPEI CLOSER. I'M MIDDLE SCHOOL AND I GUESS I'M...LESS COOL THAN OTHER KIDS. MY ORDINARY LIFE CHANGED FOREVER WHEN A SORCER CALLED ANTHONIO AND HIS DOLL CHAMOKY ATTACKED ME. TURNS OUT MY GRANDPA, WHO WENT MISSING IN AFRICA SEVERA YEARS AGO, IS ACTUALLY POWERFUL SORCERER CALLED THE "SORCERER KING."

THEY SAY IF SOMEONE EATS MY HEART, THEY GE GRANDPA'S POWERS. I THOUGHT I WAS A GONER WHEN CHAMOKY CORNERE ME... BUT HYDE, THE TEDD BEAR GRANDPA GAVE ME WHEN I WAS LITTLE, SUDDENLY CAME TO LIFE AND PROTECTED ME. GRANDPA PUT A SPELL ON HYDE JUST IN CASE SOME-THING LIKE THIS HAPPENED

AFTER THAT, OTHER SOR-CERERS AND THEIR DOLLS CAME AFTER ME. THERE W THE JACK-IN-THE-BOX HAR AWATASKY FROM RUSSIA; TRADITIONAL JAPANESE DOLL, TOMIKO, WITH HER BOYFRIEND, SHINDO; AND A MEAN SHADOW PUPPET CALLED SEYABDI WITH HIS MASTER, BUGS. HYDE PRO-TECTED ME AT FIRST, BUT ALL THOSE BATTLES TAUG ME A FEW THINGS ABOUT PROTECTING MYSELF. I THINK...

IN THE BATTLE WITH SEYABDI, MY CLASSMATE (AND GANGSTER MOVIE FANGIRL) URYU STARTED HELP ME. I ALSO WON OV SHINDO AFTER SAVING TOMIKO FOR HIM.

OUT OF THE SIX SORCER-ERS WHO SWORE TO KILL ME, ONLY FOUR ARE LEFT WHO'S COMING AFTER ME NEXT...?!

Act 14
Puppet ①

HYDE?

HUH
?

WHERE'D
HE GO?
THAT'S
WEIRD
...

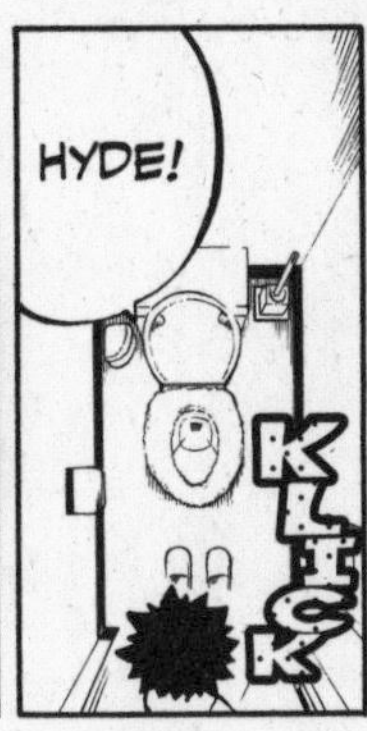
HYDE!
KLICK

HYDE!

Shun-boy.
I'm going
out.
-Hyde

UNK

?

NASU

POLICE
POLICE
POLICE

AHHH!

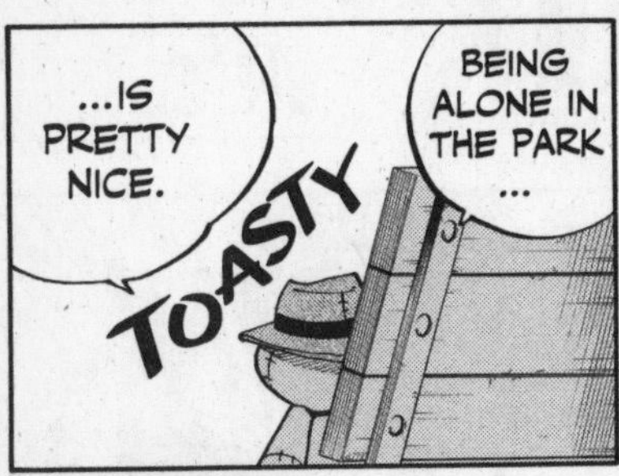
BEING ALONE IN THE PARK ...
...IS PRETTY NICE.
TOASTY

TALK
TLK

!

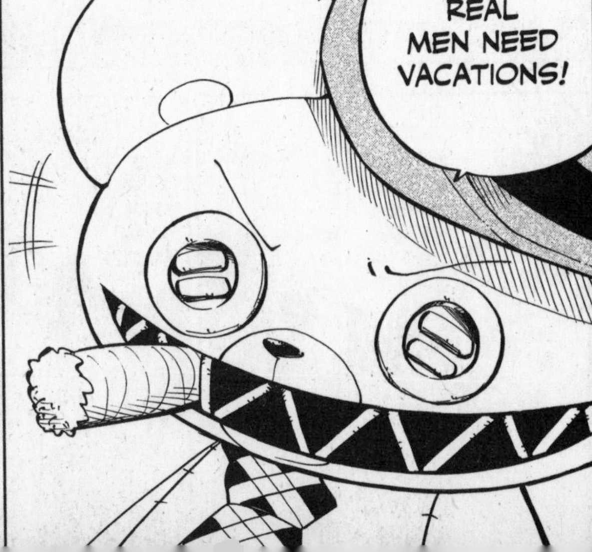
REAL MEN NEED VACATIONS!

FOUND YOU!
HYDE!
JMP
WHEEZ
WHEEZ

YOINK
WHAT GIVES, SHUN-BOY?!
SQ
WRM

I TOLD YOU NOT TO GO OUT IN PUBLIC! WHAT WERE YOU THINKING?!
IT'S A MIRACLE NOBODY SAW YOU!

A MAN'S GOTTA BE FREE.
I DON'T TAKE ORDERS FROM NOBODY!
HEHHEH
GRANDPA...
HYDE IS MORE THAN I CAN HANDLE...

MOMMY!
!

THAT GUY IS PLAYING WITH DOLLS!
SWP
MMRM

NOW, TAKU.
DON'T BE RUDE.
HAHAHA

KIDS THESE DAYS ARE UNDER A LOT OF PRESSURE.
LET'S JUST LEAVE HIM ALONE.
OK.
WAA

HYDE... WE'RE GOING HOME...
RUMBLE
Y-YEAH.

!
TLK TLK

WHAT'S WITH THAT CROWD?
IS THERE A STREET PERFORMER OR SOME-THING?

LET'S TAKE A LOOK, SHUN-BOY!
PROMISE YOU WON'T MOVE AT ALL?

PEEP

AND NOW!
PRINCESS MONICA IS HELD CAPTIVE BY THE EVIL JESTER!
WILL PRINCE ALEC BE ABLE TO SAVE HER?

IT'S A PUPPET SHOW ...
THAT'S RARE THESE DAYS.

GO, PRINCE ALEC!
BEAT THAT GUY UP!

OH, PRINCE ALEC.
OH, SAVE ME!
AIEEE
TWI RL

EVIL ALWAYS LOSES!
YOU UGLY JEST-ER!
KEEP YOUR DIRTY HANDS OFF THE PRINCESS!
KLICK

HO HO HO.
I'LL JUST BEAT YOU DOWN INSTEAD!

DON'T LOSE!
PRINCE ALEC!

HO HO HO!
KNOCK
TAKE THAT!

HO HO!
KNOCK
HAH!

AHH!
WATCH OUT, PRINCE ALEC!

HO HO!
JMP
AHHH!

HRRNG!
KLANG

HUH ...?
PRINCE... ALEC?!

KNOCK
AHHHHH!
HOHO HOHO HOHO!

KNOCK
AHHH!
HO HO HO!

KNOCK
KNOCK
KNOCK
KNOCK
KNOCK
KNOCK
I BECAME A JESTER ONLY BECAUSE I WAS BORN WITH AN UGLY FACE!
NOBODY BORN TO ROYALTY WILL EVER UNDER-STAND HOW I FEEL!
RRIP

EVIL CANNOT WIN?!
THEN *YOU* ARE THE EVIL ONE!
KRIP
WAHH
DON'T LOOK!
LET'S GO HOME!
LOSERS ARE EVIL.

GO TO HELL, EVIL PRINCE!
WAHH
HO HO!
HOHO HOHO HO!

W- WHAT IS THIS?!

AND THUS...
...THE JESTER DEFEATED THE EVIL PRINCE.
TUP!

AND LIVED HAPPILY EVER AFTER...

...WITH PRINCESS MONICA.

WOOOSH

IS HE...?!
YEAH... NEW ENEMY.

KLICK
TWITCH

ZZIP
HUH ?!

HE WANTS US TO FOLLOW HIM...?
KLICK

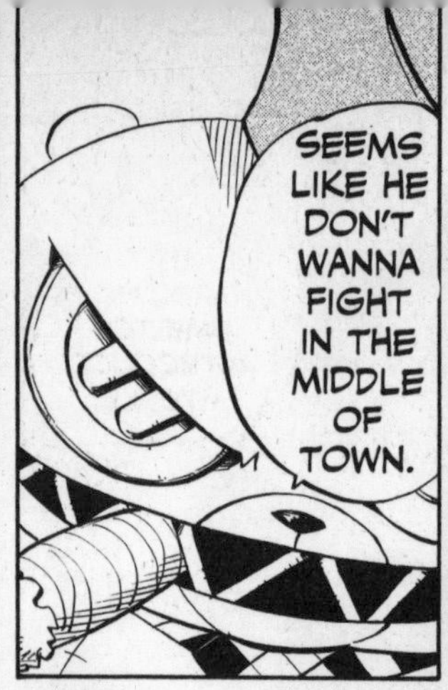
SEEMS LIKE HE DON'T WANNA FIGHT IN THE MIDDLE OF TOWN.

HEH HEH ...
LET'S SEE WHAT HE'S GOT UP HIS SLEEVE.

I AM VERY HONORED TO MEET...
...THE DESCEN-DENT...

...OF LEGEND-ARY CLOSER.
KLUP

ALLOW ME TO INTRODUCE MYSELF.

I AM KEFMAN.

I HAVE COME TODAY TO TAKE POSSESSION OF YOUR HEART, MR. CLOSER.

HO HO HO.

PLEASED TO MAKE YOUR ACQUAINT-ANCE.
GLEAM
GEEZ...
WHAT A WALK IN THE PARK THIS TURNED OUT TO BE.

LET'S OFF THIS HERE "GENTLEMAN"...
...AND HEAD HOME, SHUN-BOY!
YEAH!
ZZP

"TEXAS CHAINSAW!"

"MASSACRE MARIONETTE!"

SNAP

SNAP

ZVIP ZVIP
GLEAM
!
SHUN! GET DOWN!
?!
SLFF
KLANG
SLFF

SWFF
KRASH

WHAT...?!
THIS IS...?!

A WIRE?!
GLEAM
GLEAM

HEH...
INTEREST-ING CURSE YA GOT THERE!
HYDE...?!

"TEXAS CHAINSAW" IS A "DESTRUCTIVE" CURSE.
RUMBLE

BUT "MASSACRE MARION-ETTE"...
...IS JUST A "CUTTING" CURSE.

TOUCH THAT WIRE AND YA DIE.
WATCH IT, SHUN-BOY!
GULP

HO HO!
YOU DEDUCED MY ATTACK AFTER A SINGLE STRIKE.
WHAT AN ACCOMPLISHED FELLOW.
HOWEVER, I DOUBT YOU CAN AVOID...
...COUNTLESS WIRES COMING FROM ALL DIRECTIONS?
DON'T GET CARRIED AWAY, PUNK.

I SEE YER HAND.
KRASH
IF I CAN SEE WHERE THEY COME FROM...
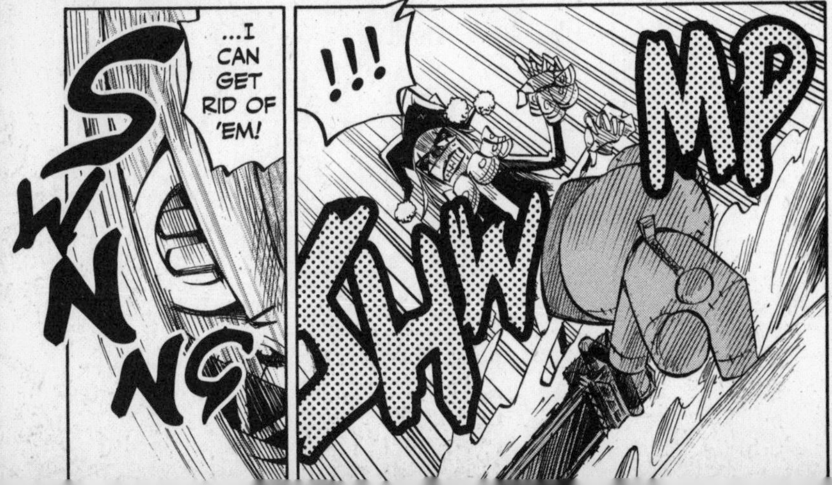
!!!
...I CAN GET RID OF 'EM!

OUCH! THAT HURTS! IT HURTS SO MUCH!
M-MY ARM!
SQ
WRM

YOU DID IT!

A... AHHHHH!

YER NOT GOOD ENOUGH.
GIVE IT UP.

HO HO!
M- ME?
OOPH
NOT GOOD ENOUGH ?
HO HO HO!
HO HO HO HO!

HO HO HO HO HO HO HO HO HO HO HO HO HO HO HO HO

W- WHAT'S WRONG WITH HIM?
HO HO HO HO
CAREFUL...! HE IS CRAZY!
HO HO HO HO

WHAT'S SO FUNNY?
HO HO HO ...

YOU TWO...
... COULD NEVER DEFEAT ME.
OOPH

BECAUSE YOU HAVE TWO...

...VERY FATAL WEAK POINTS.

TWO...
...WEAK POINTS?

Act 15
Puppet ②

COULD NEVER DEFEAT YA...

...YA SAY?

THAT IS CORRECT. BECAUSE YOU HAVE...

...TWO VERY FATAL WEAK POINTS.

WEAK POINTS ...?!

IF YER BLUFF-ING, GIVE IT A REST.

DON'T GOT TIME FER THIS.

HO HO HO ...

THEN ALLOW ME...

YOO HOO

...TO ILLUS-TRATE MY POINT!
ZVIP
ZVIP

GLEAM

GLEAM

!

SLFF

UGH!
SHUN!
KRASH

AHHH!

SHUN-BOY!

SWFF
ARE YOU OK?!
Y-YEAH. I'M FINE!

HO HO HO...
WHAT DO YOU THINK?

THE CLOSER MR. HYDE GETS TO ME...
...THE EASIER IT BECOMES TO REACH MR. CLOSER WITH THE "MASSACRE MARIONETTE."

IN OTHER WORDS...
...MR. HYDE MUST STAY NEAR MR. CLOSER DURING THE FIGHT.

WHEREAS MY SORCERER ATTACKS FROM A SAFE DISTANCE...

...YOU MUST ALWAYS PROTECT A VULNERABLE HUMAN WHILE YOU FIGHT!

THIS IS YOUR FIRST WEAK POINT!

SMASH

KRASH
ZVIP
SLFF

UGH ...!
HO HO!
YOU WOULD HAVE BEEN ABLE TO DODGE THAT ATTACK FIGHTING ALONE. BUT IT'S IMPOSSIBLE BECAUSE YOU MUST DEFEND MR. CLOSER SIMUL-TANEOUSLY.
NOW WHAT WILL YOU DO?

GLARE

HYDE!
YOWCH
JUST A SCRATCH.

BUT ...
YOINK
...THAT WEAKNESS GOES FOR YOU TOO.

TMP
SHUN-BOY!

WHY ARE YOU SO CONFIDENT ...
...WHEN YOUR SORCERER IS NEARBY TOO?
HOW IS THAT *OUR* WEAK POINT?!

I'M NOT RUNNING ANYMORE!

I CAN'T DRAG HYDE DOWN FOREVER!

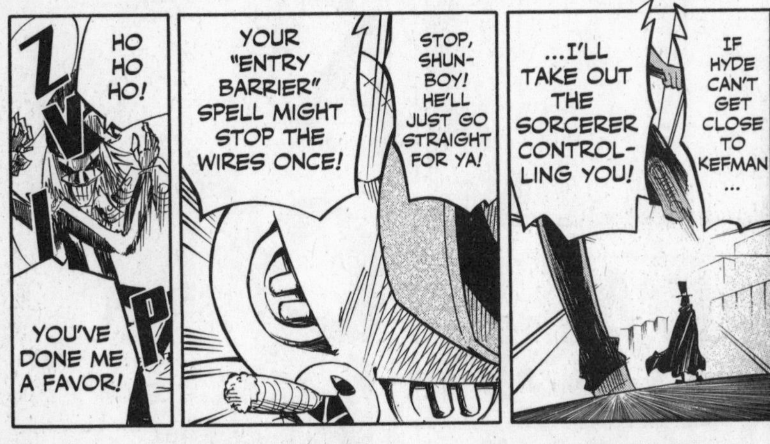
IF HYDE CAN'T GET CLOSE TO KEFMAN...
...I'LL TAKE OUT THE SORCERER CONTROL-LING YOU!
STOP, SHUN-BOY! HE'LL JUST GO STRAIGHT FOR YA!
YOUR "ENTRY BARRIER" SPELL MIGHT STOP THE WIRES ONCE!
HO HO HO!
ZVIIIP
YOU'VE DONE ME A FAVOR!

I JUST HAVE TO...
KLINK

...BLOCK THAT WIRE ONCE!
SWAA

THIS IS MY DOMAIN!
KLACK
I SAY WIRES...
...ARE NOT ALLOWED HERE!
KRASH
SMASH

KRACKLE
!!
MY WIRE ...?!
SWOO
AHHHH!
AHHHHHHHHHH!
SWACK

GRONK

HUH ?!

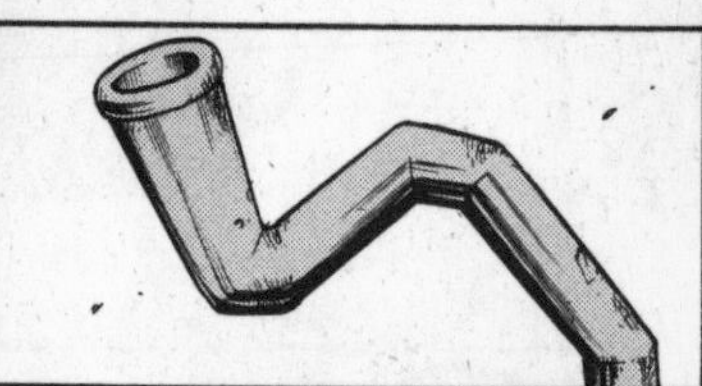

AH ...!
AHH ...
KRUSH

ACK
SW
!

SWING

AHHH!
SWFF
COUGH
UGH... AH...!
NO WAY...
COUGH
GRRP
FWAP
HE'S ACTUALLY ...
BOOM
...A PUPPET HIMSELF?!
KLICK
KLICK

HO HO HO.
DID YOU REALLY THINK...
...THAT MY SORCERER WOULD...
KOFF
KOFF
...RISK BEING HERE?
HIS NAME IS MICHELAN.
HAHAHAHA
LIKE MYSELF, HE IS A BALL-JOINTED PUPPET BEING CONTROLLED BY SORCERY.

NO...!
HOW COULD THERE BE TWO PUPPETS?!
HO HO HO.
IT SHOULDN'T BE ALL THAT SURPRISING.
CURSE DOLLS MOVE WITH THE POWER OF A SORCERER.
DEPENDING ON THE POWER OF THE SORCERER, THERE IS NO LIMIT TO HOW MANY PUPPETS HE OR SHE CAN CONTROL.
SNAP
SNAP
WOOSH

ENRIQUE, MY MASTER ...

...IS YOUNG, BUT VERY POWERFUL.

FOR HIM...

... CONTROLLING TWO PUPPETS IS SIMPLE.

POOF

TMP
HMPH ...!
SHUN-BOY!

!
I AM SORRY, BUT...
...I CANNOT ALLOW YOU TO GO NEAR MR. CLOSER.

YOU SHOULD KNOW NOW...
...HOW DIRE YOUR SITUATION IS.

AS FOR YOUR SECOND ...
...AND MOST SIGNIFICANT WEAK POINT.

SORCERERS FROM ALL OVER THE WORLD ARE OUT FOR YOUR BLOOD...

...AND YOU ARE COMPLETELY ISOLATED.

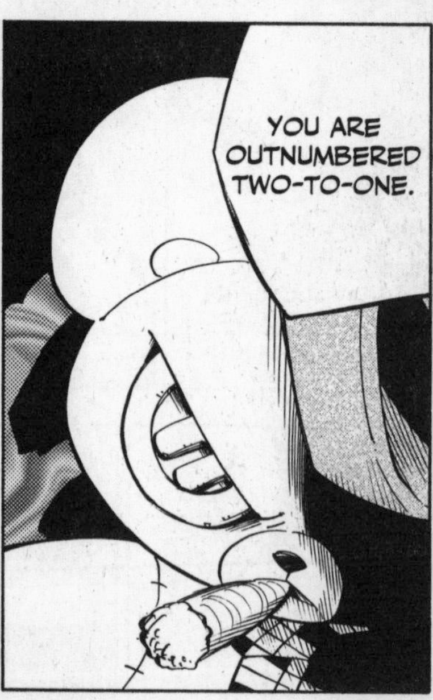
YOU ARE OUTNUMBERED TWO-TO-ONE.

AND YOU HAVE NO ONE TO HELP YOU.

MR. HYDE... REMAIN THERE.

JINGLE

UGH ...!

WATCH MR. CLOSER HAVE THE LIFE TWISTED OUT OF HIM...

AH...

DO ENJOY IT.

AHHHHH!

WOOSH

GRRP
...?!
WHAT ...?!
HAIR ...?!
YOU'RE RIGHT.
THAT PART OF YOUR PLAN ISN'T BAD.
KLICK
WHEN YOU USE TWO CURSE DOLLS, YOU CAN RENDER CLOSER TOTALLY VULNERABLE DESPITE YOUR SORCERER'S POWER BEING DIVIDED.
HOW-EVER ...
... YOU MIS-CALCULAT-ED.
SHI ...!

SHINDO ?!
CLOSER ...
...HAS ME. SOSUKE SHINDO!

CLOSER ...
...HAS ME. SOSUKE SHINDO!
FWOOOSH
Act 16 Puppet 3

SHINDO!

IT CANNOT BE.
CLOSER CAN'T POSSIBLY...
...HAVE ALLIES!

HO... HOHOHO...
MR. SHINDO... THAT IS YOUR NAME?
WHAT IS YOUR MOTIVE?

YOU ARE A SORCERER LIKE MY MASTER ENRIQUE.
YET YOU DO NOT WISH TO HAVE THE POWER OF CLOSER?

ARE YOU OK, SHUN-BOY?!
TMP
Y-YEAH, I'M FINE.
THROB

SHIN-DO...
WHAT'S GOING ON?
WHY ARE YOU HELPING US?

I'M NOT DOING THIS FOR YOU.

I'M DOING IT FOR ME.

NOT ONLY DID YOU FORGIVE MY PAST MISTAKES ...
...YOU ALSO SAVED TOMIKO'S LIFE.
THAT'S A DEBT I CAN NEVER REPAY.
SO I'M WITH YOU, CLOSER!

SHINDO ...!

SO, LET'S START OVER.
YOU'RE HAVING TROUBLE WITH THAT WIRE, RIGHT?

WE'LL TAKE CARE OF THAT JESTER PUPPET.
SHINDO ?!

MAKE IT SNAPPY.
I'VE GOT A LOT ON MY SCHEDULE TODAY.

AFTER THIS, I NEED TO GO HOME AND WRITE SOME PROPOSALS FOR STUDENT COUNCIL, THEN STUDY FOR THE FINALS, THEN I HAVE PRIVATE TUTORING AND AN ECONOMICS LESSON SO I CAN TAKE OVER MY FATHER'S BUSINESS SOMEDAY.
OH AND THERE'S ALSO CELLO AND FENCING LESSONS, THEN TEA CEREMONY, FLOWER ARRANGEMENTS, CALLIGRAPHY, AND...
O-OK! I GET IT, YOU'RE BUSY!

HO... HOHO HO!
YOU INTEND TO FIGHT ME...
...WITH THAT FILTHY HAIR?
VERY WELL! I SHALL BE YOUR OPPONENT!
"MASSACRE MARIONETTE!"
ZIP

"RELENT-
LESS
HUG!"

UGH!

SHINDO!

HO HO HO!
I DO WISH THAT YOU WOULD STOP TALKING NONSENSE.

MY "MASS-ACRE MARION-ETTE"...
...IS A CURSE SHARP ENOUGH TO CUT STEEL!

YOU INTEND TO STOP IT WITH ONLY HAIR?!
SWACK
HOW UTTERLY FOOLISH!
UGH ...!
PLIP

MY PLAN HAS SUFFERED A MILD UPSET...
... BUT THE OUTCOME WILL NOT CHANGE.
AFTER I KILL YOU, I SHALL...

... REMOVE MR. CLOSER'S HEART.

IT'S NO GOOD...!
EVEN SHINDO AND TOMIKO ...
...CAN'T HANDLE THOSE WIRES!

HYDE!
WE HAVE TO HELP!
...
THAT'LL BE TOUGH, SHUN-BOY.

CAN'T TAKE MY EYES OFF HIM.
HA HA HA
HE'S JUST WAITIN' TO TWIST THE LIFE OUT OF YA, SHUN.
HOO HOO HOO

BUT... IF WE JUST...!
STEADY, SHUN-BOY.

THEY WON'T LOSE THAT EASY.

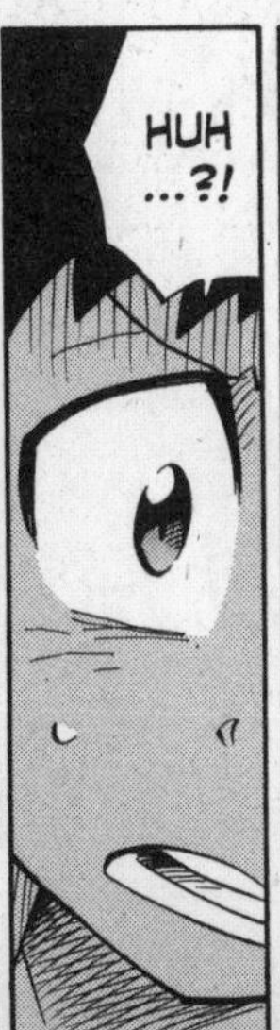
HUH ...?!

HYDE IS CORRECT.

WE'VE CHANGED SINCE MEETING YOU.

I'LL MAKE TOMIKO HUMAN...
...WITHOUT THE POWER OF CLOSER'S BLOODLINE.

BELIEVING IN OUR LOVE...
...HAS MADE US STRONGER THAN EVER.

LET ME SHOW YOU.
IS THAT ...?!
THE SPELL OF ETERNAL LOVE...!
SHN
GNN
"CRIMSON BRIDE!"

!
HUH ...!
TO...
TOMIKO ...
... TURNED HUMAN ?!
SIR CLOSER. SIR HYDE.
GOOD DAY TO YOU.
TH...
THAT'S AMAZ-ING!
AWE-SOME, SHINDO!

WOBBLE
EH? EH?

SH-SHINDO?!
HE'S OLD?!
EH...?

WHASSA? EH? BAH! WHASSA-MANA SEGWENNA, EH? BAH!
"THE 'CRIMSON BRIDE' SPELL ISN'T COMPLETE YET. IT CONSUMES ALMOST ALL OF MY POWER TO USE THIS SPELL AND IT MAKES ME LOOK OLD WHEN I DO."
HOW DO YOU KNOW?!
THAT IS WHAT HE IS SAYING.

MASTER SHINDO...
SWAA
EH?
EH?

!
PLIP

YOUR POWERS MAY HAVE INCREASED ...
ZVIP

HO HO HO!
WHAT A STRANGE SPELL THAT IS!
BUT IT'S LACKING IN SUB-STANCE.
GLARE

...HOWEVER, YOUR HAIR...
... CANNOT WIN AGAINST WIRES!
SHWING

HALT!!

WHAT?!

WHAT IS THIS ...?!
GRRP
THE HAIR?!
GRRP

HOW IS THIS POSSIBLE ...?!
MY WIRES...
...STOPPED BY A SINGLE STRAND OF HAIR ?!
IMPOS-SIBLE!
INCON-CEIVABLE!
THIS CANNOT BE HAPPEN-ING!

THE ONLY REASON YOU WILL LOSE TO ME...
SLINK
SLINK
...IS THE FACT THAT...
...I LOVE MASTER SHINDO.
SLINK

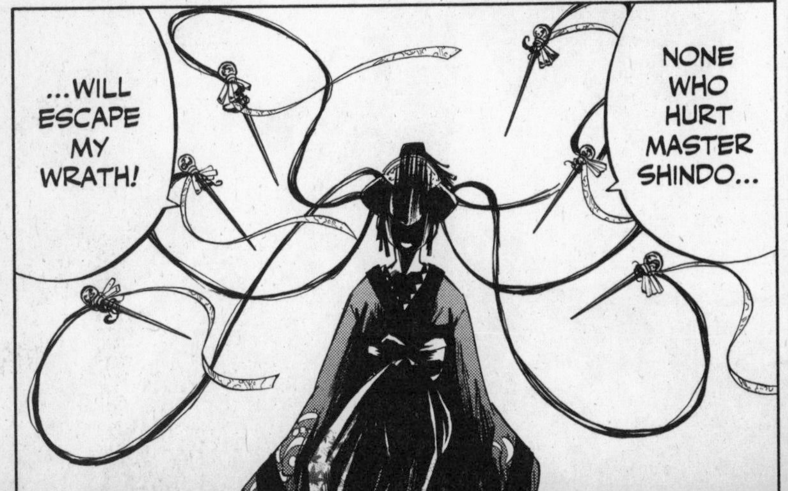
NONE WHO HURT MASTER SHINDO...
...WILL ESCAPE MY WRATH!

KRASH

HOW ...?!
HOW COULD I FAIL...
...TO CUT THAT SINGLE STRAND OF HAIR...?
KRASH

HEH HEH...
EH? WHASHAYA-NAMAHADA ...

"THIS HAIR BINDS MY LOVE TO TOMIKO."
"SOMEONE LIKE YOU COULD NEVER SEVER IT."

...IS...
EH?
WASSA?
...WHAT MASTER SHINDO SAID.

DOOM
Act 17
Puppet 4

N-NO WAY!

KEFMAN IS MY MASTER-PIECE!

HOW'D HE LOSE TO A JAPANESE DOLL?!

H- HE'S SO STRONG!
HE'S WAY STRONGER THAN WHEN WE FOUGHT!

SO COOL!
SHINDO!
TOMIKO!
IT WAS NOTHING.
EH?
EH!
SHAKE
PEACE

...!
IT'S OK...
I STILL HAVE MICHE-LAN!
I'LL JUST REDIRECT POWER FROM KEFMAN TO MICHELAN...
...AND FIGHT WITH JUST ONE PUPPET!
KREAK

WHAT WILL YOU DO, HYDE?
!

IF IT PLEASES YOU, I SHALL DEAL WITH THE REMAINING ONE AS WELL ...

NO THANKS, DOLL-FACE.
CAN'T HAVE YOU...
...DOING ALL THE MEN'S WORK.
HMPH

YA HEAR THAT, YA BIG OAF?
JUST YOU AND ME! ONE ON ONE!
HA HA HA HA

TMP TMP

LET'S FINISH THIS!
SW WNG

RUUUU

SMASH!

5

W- WHAT WAS THAT?!
HYDE'S "TEXAS CHAINSAW" ...
...!
...HE JUST...
HAHAHA
HOO HOO
... DODGED IT!
HA... HAHA!
THAT'S RIGHT!
THIS IS MICHE-LAN'S CURSE!
BOXING, KUNG FU, JUJUTSU, SAMBO...
HE'S A "MASSACRE PUPPET," MASTER OF ALL KINDS OF MARTIAL ARTS!
HE CAN DEFLECT ANY ATTACK...
...AND HIS FISTS ARE PURE POWER!

THINGS AREN'T WORKING OUT LIKE I PLANNED...
...BUT I DON'T NEED A PLAN TO BEAT YOU!

THAT CHAINSAW WON'T WORK ON MICHELAN!
I'LL MESS YOU UP SO BAD...
...NO-BODY WILL RECOG-NIZE YOU!
WOOSH
A MARTIAL ARTS...
...EXPERT...

...EH?

SO WHAT?

SMASH

HA HA
HOO HOO
KRASK

HUH ?!

IF YER GOOD AT DODGING ...

HA HA
...I JUST GOTTA HIT BACK ...
SHWING

KRASH
...WHEN YOU ATTACK.
HAHA
HOO HOO
NO WAY!
MICHE-LAN'S FISTS ...!
SORRY, BUT BRUTE STRENGTH IS MY SPECIALTY.
MAN-TO-MAN...
...A PUNK LIKE YOU'S GOT NOTHING...
...ON OLD MAN CLOSER.
IT'S MORE'N YOU CAN HANDLE.
SEE YA.
IMP

KRASH
HE DID IT!
WAY TO GO, HYDE!
N-NO...!
MICHE-LAN WAS...
...DE-FEATED, TOO?!
THIS IS BAD.
MY "CURSE"...
...IS GOING TO BOUNCE BACK ON ME!
KREAK

KHA CK!!
!
A-AHHHHH!
UGH!
!
SHUN-BOY?!

SWFFF

WHY DID YOU...?!
OW! THAT HURT!
OUCH
THROB
THROB

WHY DID YOU HELP ME?
I TRIED...

...TO KILL YOU!
...

I KNOW.
BUT YOU COULD'VE DIED IF YOU FELL FROM THERE.

THAT'S KIND OF A HARSH PUNISHMENT...

...FOR A KID WHO MADE A MISTAKE.

WAY TOO SOFT...

THAT'S CLOSER'S SPECIALTY.

Back to normal

WELL THAT TURNED OUT TO BE A LONG WALK.
LET'S GO HOME, SHUN-BOY.
YEAH.
HUH ...?
H-HEY!

SHINDO, TOMIKO ...
THANKS SO MUCH FOR THE HELP.
DON'T MENTION IT.
YOU CAN COUNT ON US.

IF THEY KEEP COMIN' LIKE THIS ...
...I WON'T BE ABLE TO GO FOR WALKS.
SERIOUS-LY.
I WONDER WHO STARTED THIS THING ABOUT EATING MY HEART ...

...TO GET CLOSER'S POWER.
...
I KNOW WHO.
HUH ?

I MET THE MAN WHO TOLD US ALL THAT.

THE MAN WHO SENT ALL THE SORCERERS IN THE WORLD AFTER YOU.

HUH ...?!
WHAT DID YOU SAY?!

MY FATHER DIED...
...AND MY MOM GOT A BAD HEART FROM WORRYING SO MUCH.

I WAS BORN WITH A TALENT FOR SORCERY...
...SO I TELL OTHER PEOPLE'S FORTUNES...
...AND FIND STUFF THEY LOST, TO MAKE A LIVING.
BUT...

IT'S NOT ENOUGH!
THIS WON'T PAY FOR MOM'S HEART SURGERY!
FWIP
KLANG
WHAT SHOULD I DO?!
THAT WAS WHEN...
...ALL OF A SUDDEN...
...THAT MAN APPEARED IN A WINDOW.
YOU'RE A SORCER-ER.
!

IT WAS LIKE THIS MAGIC SPACE OPENED UP AND HE WAS SITTING THERE IN A WINDOW, STARING AT ME...
HE STARTED TALKING TO ME QUIETLY!
IT SEEMS ...
...YOU HAVE TALENT.
BUT YOUR POWERS ...
...ARE WASTED WITH SUCH PETTY MATTERS.
LET ME TELL YOU SOMETHING.
SOMETHING THAT WILL BRING YOU WONDERFUL POWER ...
...THAT CAN GRANT ANY WISH .
LATER I HEARD ...
...THAT THAT MAN APPEARS ALL OVER THE WORLD.
HE'S CALLED ...

...THE WATCHER IN THE WINDOW.

BONUS COMIC
Aso's Horror Theater!

ONE MORNING, ASO WOKE UP...
...AND NOTICED SOMETHING WAS WRONG. HIS EAR...
Hello

...WAS BLEEDING PROFUSELY ...!
WHAT'S GOING ON?!
Hello
PLUP

BLEEDING FROM THE EAR SOUNDS REALLY SCARY.
Yes, this is BAD.
Hello

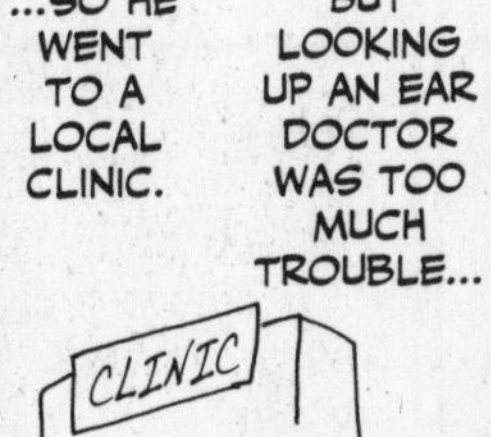
BUT LOOKING UP AN EAR DOCTOR WAS TOO MUCH TROUBLE...
...SO HE WENT TO A LOCAL CLINIC.
CLINIC
Hello

THE DOCTOR, WHO WAS PROBABLY GERMAN, SPOKE IN BROKEN JAPANESE, SAYING...
I GOT NO IDEA.
THAT'S ALL HE SAID.
OK.

MY GRAND-FATHER'S EARS BLEED.

COULD THIS BE...?!
Hello

AFTER HEARING SOME OLD DUDE TALK ENDLESSLY IN HIS RASPY VOICE, I FEEL LIKE I'M BLEEDING FROM THE EARS...

THAT'S NOT IT!
Hello

I POKED MY EAR TOO HARD WITH A Q-TIP AND IT STARTED BLEEDING! OOPS!

NOT IT!
Hello

BUT HE WAS STILL WORRIED, SO AFTER GOING HOME...

...HE WENT ON THE INTERNET AND SEARCHED FOR "BLEEDING FROM THE EAR."

KLICK

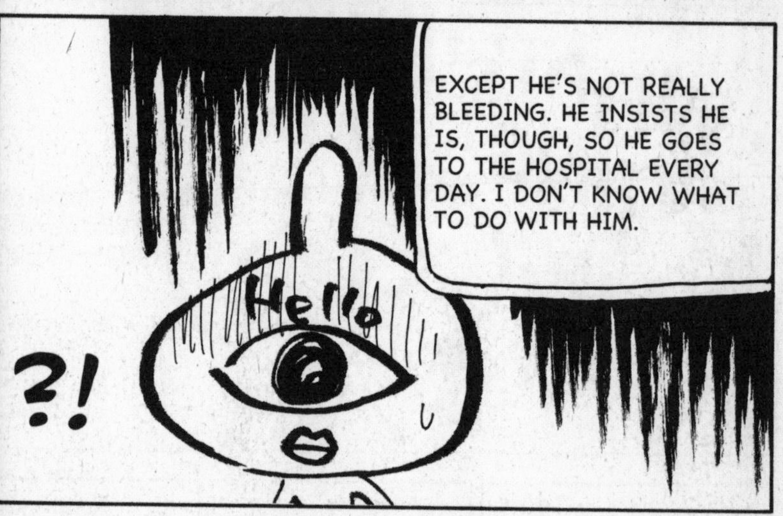
EXCEPT HE'S NOT REALLY BLEEDING. HE INSISTS HE IS, THOUGH, SO HE GOES TO THE HOSPITAL EVERY DAY. I DON'T KNOW WHAT TO DO WITH HIM.
?!
Hello

IS THIS REALLY IT?!

IS THIS IT?

COULD ASO BE THE SAME ...?!

IS THAT IT?

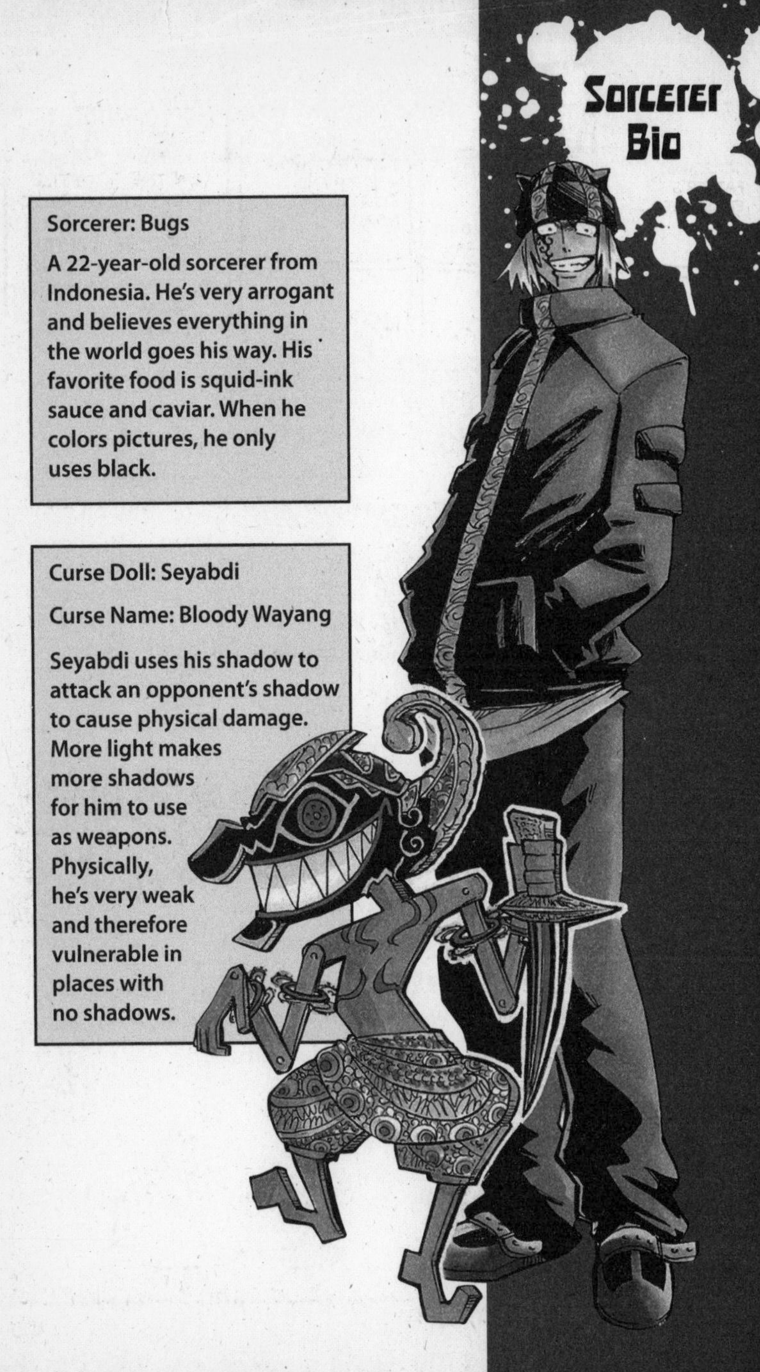
Sorcerer
Bio
Sorcerer: Bugs
A 22-year-old sorcerer from Indonesia. He's very arrogant and believes everything in the world goes his way. His favorite food is squid-ink sauce and caviar. When he colors pictures, he only uses black.
Curse Doll: Seyabdi
Curse Name: Bloody Wayang
Seyabdi uses his shadow to attack an opponent's shadow to cause physical damage. More light makes more shadows for him to use as weapons. Physically, he's very weak and therefore vulnerable in places with no shadows.

Haro Aso

Hello! This is Aso!
Volume 2 is out! It's been a quick six months since the serialization started. Time flies. At this rate, I might become an old man without noticing... But I guess I wouldn't mind if I turned out like Shunpei's grandpa. Anyway, keep on enjoying Shunpei's coming-of-age journey!